Alan has given us the step-by-step approach to truly looking at our donor base. It is needed by many not for profits across the United States.

Duana Linville Dralus
President of the Board
Mid Continent Council, Girl Scouts

Where this book seems to me to differ from many books about marketing is in its specificity. The advice and guidelines that it offers are clear, crisp and specific. The ideas contained in this book can be of enormous help across a wide range of industries. The non-profit performing arts world would benefit a great deal from applying the principles found here.

Henry Fogel
President,
American Symphony Orchestra League

This book contains many key components of things that must be understood to run beneficial marketing programs. Worth conscientious usage.

Barnett C. Helzberg, Jr.
Former owner of Helzberg Diamonds
Author, *What I Learned Before I Sold to Warren Buffet*

Data-Driven Business Models offers unique insight into database marketing. Alan Weber created a "how to book" that methodically takes you step by step through a rational process and the benefits of change. This book is more than analytics, it is an entrepreneurial treatise fully exploring the direct linkage between customers, business models, teams and the need for measuring execution.

Thomas H. Holcom Jr.
VP Pioneer Financial Group
Founder, Angel Flight Central

Alan Weber's knowledge of database marketing is based on many years of hands-on experience. He also writes extremely well. His explanations avoid jargon and concentrate on getting his points across very clearly so that readers can understand them. There are few experts in the industry who have both the experience and writing skill of Alan Weber. His new book, *Data-Driven Business Models* is great. I love it. I can highly recommend *Data-Driven Business Models* to anyone who wants to understand the marketing industry today.

Arthur Middleton Hughes, Vice President / Solutions Architect, KnowledgeBase Marketing, and author of
Strategic Database Marketing 2nd Ed. (McGraw Hill 2000)

Almost every busy person I know wants to find "the answer" on how to best grow their business. However, so few take the time to look for those answers in a systematic way. Even fewer have the ability to take those answers and put them into action. In his new book *Data-Driven Business Models* Alan Weber gives business leaders the information they need to set about building their organizations in a logical and strategic manner. From the latest in business modeling to customer value indexing, Alan's book delivers what business leaders must know in order to achieve sustained success.

Like Peter Drucker said, "Marketing is everything." Drucker would love this book.

Steve S. Little
Senior Consultant, *Inc.* magazine

"Alan Weber has written the definitive "how-to" political bible for implementing a database marketing program. An essential read for any business that is trying to revamp their current database operations and systems. He shares his war stories and his tactics for successful campaigns to win the war in database marketing. Alan's keen insight and careful observations come from years of experience in the trenches of database operations. Reading the book is akin to having your own database consultant by your side!"

Pegg Nadler
Pegg Nadler Associates, Inc.
Chair of the 2003–2004 Direct Marketing Association
Non-Profit Federation Advisory Council

This comprehensive book offers a broad scoped introduction to the use of data driven decisioning. The author offers a seamless blend of direct marketing subjects with real life examples. This book is a must for your library.

Kurtis M. Ruf
Ruf Strategic Solutions

Finally, a text that describes, defines and illustrates the 'missing link' for most organizations—the business model. Unless everyone understands the business model being used, confusion usually reigns. This text ties the entire organization together with a clear, cohesive, easy-to-understand management model.

Don Schultz
Professor Emeritus
Northwestern University

Data-Driven Business Models

Alan Weber

THOMSON

Australia · Brazil · Canada · Mexico · Singapore · Spain · United Kingdom · United States

Data-Driven Business Models
Alan Weber

Consulting Editor in Marketing:
Richard Hagle

Composed by: Sans Serif Inc.

Printed in the United States of America by R.R. Donnelley

1 2 3 4 5 08 07 06 05
This book is printed on acid-free paper.

ISBN: 0-324-22233-5

This publication is designed to provide accurate and authoritative information in regard to the subject matter covered. It is sold with the understanding that the publisher is not engaged in rendering legal, accounting, or other professional services. If expert assistance is required, the services of a competent professional person should be sought.

Library of Congress Cataloging in Publication Number is available. See page 279 for details.

For more information about our products, contact us at:

Thomson Learning Academic Resource Center
1-800-423-0563

Thomson Higher Education
5191 Natorp Boulevard
Mason, Ohio 45040
USA

Contents

CHAPTER 9:
Case Studies   **241**

Acknowledgments

Thanks go out to my partners, Boris and John, for putting up with me while I labored on this book, to Clayton Christensen, for sparking the ideas that started the book, to Merlin Spencer, for his help getting it going, and especially to Trish, Andrew, Catharine, and Alex, for allowing me the mental and physical time away.

Preface

This book is intended for people who want to use data to drive change at the strategic level. People who ask big questions, like "What business are we really in?" and who are not afraid of real answers, like "Not the one everyone thought we were in—and here is why."

It is also for people who want to back up their decisions with facts, but who can't seem to find the right facts in accounting, finance, IT, or marketing, or from a vendor. For many, this book will show a new way to look at business and ways to find solutions to problems they have struggled with for years.

This book is quite different than a book about marketing research, IT, or finance, but it employs a little from each. You don't have to be a technical expert in these fields to enjoy this book. A basic business background should be enough to grasp most of the concepts.

Actually, this book was written largely out of frustration. Most businesses seek to employ computers and database technology to do the same things better, but if they succeed at creating better information systems, they instead find they need to do different things.

This generates all manner of human and emotional challenges. Marketing sets out to find out more about their customers, only to discover their basic ideas about whom they should sell to are wrong. IT seeks to design systems to help managers ask questions, only to find managers need systems to know which questions to ask. Investors support a business they think is going in the right direction, only to find that business must completely change direction in order to survive.

As a result, improved information doesn't solve old problems it merely changes them. While the idea of discovering that doing different things may be better, changing what an organization does requires changing what an organization is. That kind of change can alter everything from job descriptions to compensation plans. And that results in all sorts of human and emotional challenges.

At its core, business modeling is really change management, based on facts and facilitated by people who rely on data coming out of improved reports that are supplied by database technology.

Note that I say "based on facts." This book focuses on what people do, not just what they say. Unlike approaches that emphasize survey research, this book focuses on using the tactical knowledge gained from tracking and analyzing actual buyer behavior over time.

At its core, the book is based around a single principle, which is behavior is the best predictor of behavior. Constant tracking of stimulus and response in the marketplace is the key. Paying attention to what people, customers, and prospects do through database techniques is the most effective way to judge any business model.

I hope this book helps you avoid some of the frustrations so many have confronted when trying to use data to drive change.

Business Models: What They Are, How They Work, Why They Are Important

Business model has been a hot term in business circles in recent years. Venture capitalists no longer invest in an idea or an innovation or a new strategy. When they support a start-up, they fund the business model. And when terms become hot, they inevitably become subject to misuse, abuse, and oversimplification.

So what is a business model? In simplest terms, it is that collection of characteristics, forces, and strategies that determine how a company makes a profit on its activities, in other words, how it makes money. At first glance it would appear that a business model is what the company *does,* yet it is more. It is also what the company *is.*

Elements of a Business Model

A business model is shorthand to describe how an enterprise works. It represents the nexus of an organization's strategy, internal resources, and external environment. This combination of elements of both internal and external variables is only partially controllable, but it most certainly can be managed.

The business model is managed primarily through strategic guidance. The conflict is that strategy is generally long-term, while the business model changes or is changed frequently at the tactical level, typically in response to short-term internal and external pressures.

Internal resources are something organizations can manage and they offer a means to purposely affect the business model. However, organizations often have a misperception of themselves, their customers, and how their customers respond to them, which affects their ability to set an effective strategy.

Consider a company that sells holiday gift baskets to both consumers and businesses. The people selling to businesses consistently targeted companies with 50 or more employees, hoping for a large order. Despite several years of following this strategy, 80 percent of their corporate business came from companies with 15 or fewer employees. It turned out they were more successful selling to smaller companies that gave gifts to clients than pursuing larger companies that gave gifts to employees.

So, despite a stated strategy of pursuing larger companies—their selling strength—and their determined efforts, they found that smaller companies provided most of their sales. Their internal strength and resources were best attuned to selling to smaller companies. Therefore, their business model—how they made a profit—was in fact quite different than what they thought it was, and quite different than what their strategy, had it been successful, would have created.

The environment can have a similar impact on strategy. Walgreens, a drugstore retailer, has adopted a strategy that calls for locating stores near competitors. It is not unusual to see a new Walgreens built across the street from an Osco Drug, a similar retailer. Consider how this affects Osco's business model. Osco can have a successful store without a nearby competitor for years, then a Walgreens opens across the street, immediately altering how that store conducts its business (its business model), whether the Osco home office likes it or not and whether Osco otherwise chooses to change strategy or not.

These two examples demonstrate how the environment rarely cooperates with people trying to pursue a given strategy. A changing environment creates and destroys opportunities for many business models. Organizations that can weave the right responses to those changes into timely adjustments in strategy are most likely to prosper.

Business Modeling and Business Models

In the most basic sense, businesses derive their product input, i.e., their raw materials, from at least one acquisition channel. A farmer has land on which to grow crops, wholesalers buy directly from manufacturers and sell at a higher price to retailers, service companies rely on labor, and so on. These inputs go through a value-added process, such as harvesting, packaging, manufacturing, or distribution. The goods or services are then distributed or sold through one or more wholesale, retail, or direct channels to customers.

Business modeling is the process of consciously developing and managing the enterprise's business model. Business modeling as a management technique employs the use of facts (hard data) and cross-silo cooperation. It is not a process that one department, such as marketing or production, can follow on its own, and it must be driven by top management.

Business modeling is by its very nature strategic, as it involves understanding the overall picture of the enterprise, setting or changing corporate focus, and driving change down through tactical and day-to-day implementation. For example, while a sales force may have the tactical focus of selling to large businesses, top management may make the strategic decision to create a new sales channel selling by phone and website to smaller businesses. Top management decides to alter the business model and then directs lower-level managers to implement the tactics necessary to manage their portion of the business model.

In this example, top management directs the sales force to focus on larger, not smaller businesses and creates a new team to sell to smaller, not larger businesses. It also becomes the duty of top managers initiating such strategic changes to settle inevitable squabbles among managers that may have conflicts at the tactical level. Someone must decide which customers should be targeted by which group, what to do when responsibilities overlap, and how each group is compensated for success. That someone is top management.

Top management sets the strategy—the "what to do," and leaves tactics—the "how to do it" to managers in each area. Top management need not specify which salesperson calls on which account or how telesales should prioritize their contacts. This allows top management to stay focused on strategy and driving the business model.

Fact-Based Decision Making

Sound decisions are based on facts. The very reasons for making a change in strategy invariably result from evidence, e.g., the *fact* of declining sales, that the current strategy isn't working. Indeed, building decision-making trigger points around facts gathered by the company makes it possible for managers to readily adopt changes they would otherwise reject.

The most accurate portion of the corporate knowledge in an organization is primarily contained in transactional data. This information, which drives accounting, finance, production, and sales tracking, makes up the core set of facts an organization can possess. The best information an organization has will be captured at the point of sale. Decision-makers using this data to support decisions make use of the organization's best behavioral experience. Consider the question this way: Would you rather have an experienced surgeon or a clever surgeon operate on you? Clever managers who ignore this behavioral experience do so at their peril.

Rather than uncovering "secrets," fact-based decision-makers usually uncover basic principles and relationships. It is not a matter of identifying which tree is in the forest; it is a matter of telling the forest from the trees.

The key to successful fact-based decision-making is not simply the capture of facts as data, but the relationship of that data. The relationship of various data is a function of a database. Pieces of the puzzle lie in different data systems, across different departments, and arrive from different sources. A database can tie all of that disparate information together into one logical, coherent whole.

Creating this logical, coherent whole is neither a minor task nor a foregone conclusion. The fact that data exist in a system does not mean the data are correct. For example, product cost data in a system built for salespeople may not be accurate. Salespeople often inaccurately or incompletely capture pieces of data not central to the financial portion of a transaction. Such data might never be used and therefore could be maintained inaccurately for years, without anyone's knowledge.

While responses to surveys, focus groups, and questionnaires can provide useful insights into customer attitudes and dispositions, they alone should not be used to make strategic planning decisions. Too many organizations ignore the transactional, behavior-based facts they capture when it comes to making strategic decisions. If factual, behavior-based data that already exist are contradictory to data gathered

Exhibit 1.1: Percent of Survey Respondents by Age Range of Customers

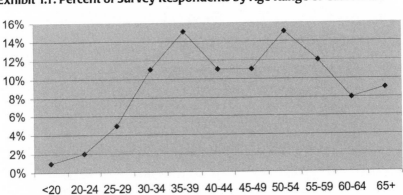

Exhibit 1.2: Percent of Customers by Age Range Based on Driver's License Registration

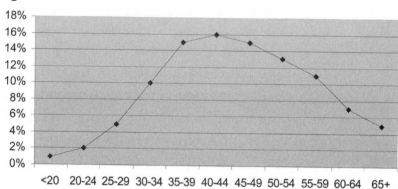

through opinion research, the opinion research should be reevaluated, as the following example illustrates.

Consider the industry that supports woodworking hobbyists in North America. Magazines such as *Wood, American Woodworker,* and *Fine Woodworking* describe projects and tools to millions of consumers that buy countless Ryobi, Dewalt, Black & Decker, and other tools.

One manufacturer of woodworking tools, American WoodWorking Tools, wanted to improve its own market knowledge. They had done several thousand surveys, similar to those done by the major woodworking magazines. A common question among the surveys concerned age. Survey responders often left the age field blank, but their results were similar to each of the magazines: Many woodworkers were in their 30s, fewer in their 40s, and many in their 50s, with a still sizable number over 65.

The common wisdom in the industry (reflected in the surveys) was that the age curve had a "double-hump," peaking in the 30s and 50s. (See Exhibit 1.1.) However, marketing management at American Wood-Working Tools took their actual customer list and compared it to driver's license registrations to determine actual age of all customers. What they found was that there was no "double-hump" at all. (See Exhibit 1.2.) People in their 40s were simply less likely to tell their age on a survey. In addition, the company had a smaller proportion of customers over age 65 than they had suspected. Apparently, older individuals were simply more likely to return the survey.

This knowledge changed the company's perception of its customers and provided it an enormous competitive advantage. American Wood-Working Tools was better able to focus on the real marketplace, unlike its competitors, who focused their energy on trying to fix a problem that didn't exist (losing customers in their 40s) and who over-emphasized marketing efforts to seniors.

Cross-Silo Cooperation

A key province of top management is a cross-silo viewpoint of the organization. This is crucial because cross-silo integration rarely occurs organically. Individual departments may not need to share resources or data; they may interact only in strictly tactical situations. Often, they view themselves as competing for resources within the organization and may consider what is good for another department to be bad for their own department.

Internal competition must be proactively controlled by top management. For example, a field sales force that is given hundreds of clients or prospects for each salesperson may be unable to give each one the attention they need and may focus only on a few large clients. However, adding a telesales department to handle smaller clients and field sales is likely to be resisted by field sales, regardless of whether or not it is good for the organization as a whole. It is the duty of top management to resolve such disputes on behalf of the entire organization.

Changes involving the information technology (IT) department often produce similar reactions. Part of IT's duties are to store and control corporate data. Giving another department, whether it is marketing, sales, or purchasing, de-centralized control of their own data is often perceived as a threat. As a result, IT will resist any effort by another department to have "their own database."

The following is an example that incorporates both obstacles. The head of marketing for a business-to-business seller of equipment calling on retailers nationwide wanted a database of customers. The database would show the various contacts at each location, who bought what, and how much they spent. The IT department was working on a new system that ultimately would answer everyone's questions, but top management was reorganizing the sales force and needed some quick answers to some of their questions.

As a result, marketing was allowed to quickly build a database separate from what IT was building. What they found was remarkable: Salespeople had hundreds of accounts on the books, but no salesperson had more than 20 large accounts. The remainder of the accounts made virtually no purchases and received virtually no contact.

Marketing proposed contacting selected medium-sized accounts directly. Initial results were encouraging. It was highly profitable to target certain accounts directly.

However, IT was almost ready with their new system, and salespeople didn't want marketing to target some of their customers, or at least some of their potential customers. So, despite successful use, the marketing system was shelved. Top management chose to fold under the specter of a turf war rather than guide the needs of the company as a whole. Three years later, the new system IT created still did not integrate sales and marketing, and it was unable to support the kind of targeting that marketing could do before with its own database.

The alternative top management response is painfully simple: If the integration had been driven from the top, an entire new sales and marketing system could have been developed. A "skunkworks" incorporating sales, marketing, and IT—a cross-silo team—could have been created to develop a program based on marketing's initial experiment. Small accounts that were uneconomical for reps to call on directly could have been serviced by some combination of telesales and direct mail. Such accounts might have been profiled to identify similar new accounts as the targets of a lead generation program, which would have been more efficient and profitable because it would have been more targeted. As accounts grew in sales volume and profitability, they could have been turned over to individual reps with some sort of bonus or override for the telesales rep who initially developed the account.

Types of Business Models

Business model structures describe, in the most basic terms possible, how goods and/or services are acquired, where value is added, and how they are distributed or sold.

Exhibits 1.3, 1.4, and 1.5 represent the basic structures of acquisition and distribution channel(s) and show how value is added in the process. The differences in acquisition and distribution channels account for the major structural differences among business models. Organizations sharing a similar value-added process tend to differ primarily in acquisition or in sales and distribution channels, i.e., they might differ in where they make their money, but not how they make it. Organizations with different value-added processes tend to have very different business models, i.e., they might use the same or similar acquisitions and sale channels but differ significantly in how they earn their money.

Four Basic Business Model Structures

To begin describing the business models, we first describe in a very basic way how things are acquired, processed, and sold. Initially, the business model should be simple and easily understood. From that point, more detailed information can be added through the business modeling process.

The structure of a business model represents, in the simplest terms, the value network the company manages to turn inputs (acquisitions) into revenue. Every business model has one of the following structures:

1. Simple
2. Convergent
3. Divergent
4. Compound

A *simple business model* has:

- One input/acquisition channel
- A common processing channel
- One output/sales channel

One example of a simple business model is a farmer who grows his own crops, brings them to his roadside stand at the edge of his farm, and sells them to neighbors and passers-by. A simple business model is represented by the diagram in Exhibit 1.3.

Exhibit 1.3: Simple Business Model

Many organizations begin with a simple business model: a single source of supply, a single process, a single market. As a company grows, it often needs to add sources of supply and needs to find new markets to sell to.

A *convergent business model* has:

- At least two input/acquisition channels
- A common processing channel
- One output/sales channel

A convergent business model can be represented by the diagram in Exhibit 1.4. The example of our farmer in the previous example could also be an example of a convergent business model if the farmer grows his own crops and also acquires pies from a neighbor. He brings both his

Exhibit 1.4: Convergent Business Model

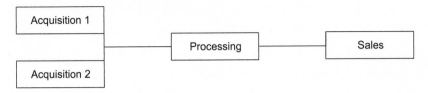

crops and his neighbor's pies to his roadside stand at the edge of his farm and sells them to neighbors and passers-by.

A convergent business model is a logical extension of a simple business model and examples are everywhere. As organizations grow, they often find they can sell more products to their customers. This can necessitate new supply sources. Consider the gas station that becomes a gas station *and* convenience store. In addition to acquiring products from an oil company, they also need to acquire groceries from one or more wholesale suppliers. However, they still sell in basically the same way.

A *divergent business model* has:

- One input/acquisition channel
- A common processing channel
- At least two output/sales channels

Return to our farmer: He grows his own crops, brings them to his stand at the edge of his farm, sells some to neighbors and passers-by, and then sells the rest to wholesalers in bulk. This kind of divergent business model is represented by the diagram in Exhibit 1.5.

Some organizations find that their customer base has such differing segments that they should be sold through different channels. For

Exhibit 1.5: Divergent Business Model

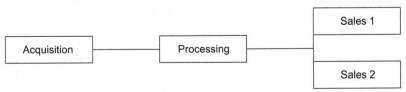

example, hardware stores have different salespeople, different checkout counters, and different types of credit accounts for contractors than they do for consumers. In many cases, the differences in the customer base exists long before the organization changes the sales methodology to take advantage if it.

A *compound business model* has:

- At least two input/acquisition channels
- A common processing channel
- At least two output/sales channels

A compound business model is a combination of convergent and divergent models. That is, it has both multiple input channels and multiple output channels.

For convergent or compound business models, there can be many acquisition channels. There can be two, three, or even 20 different acquisition channels. What separates convergent and compound from simple business models is that there is more than one acquisition channel. Exhibit 1.6 illustrates a compound business model.

Exhibit 1.6: Compound Business Model

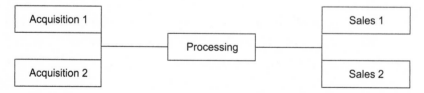

Most organizations have a compound business model. They acquire through more than one channel and sell through more than one channel. The most common way for an organization to alter the business model is to add or eliminate acquisition or sales channels.

Knowing your organization's business model is akin to, in the words of Theodore Leavitt, "knowing what business you are really in," i.e., how you make money. Often many managers are surprised to learn that they have many profitable customers in places that do not fit their conception of their business model. Knowing one's business model makes it possible to articulate and execute strategy more effectively, to compete more tenaciously, and to change more swiftly, and with minimal disruption to operations and profits.

Autonomous Business Models

Basic business models can assume a single common processing or value-added operation for varying numbers of acquisition and sales channels. However, this is not always the case. For example, a conglomerate such as General Electric has fourteen separate business units that do not really interact on a regular basis. The business model of the division selling electric light bulbs is entirely different and entirely separate from the business model of the division selling locomotives, which is entirely different from the entertainment division, and so on.

It is important to recognize when business models are autonomous. The fact that data may pass through the same computer does not mean the products, services, sales channels, or customers are related.

Autonomous business models don't directly affect each other on the operational level, but they do compete on an important level: They compete for the attention of top management, they compete for corporate capital resources, and, depending on the resolution of these first two areas of competition, they may or may not provide an advantage for each other in the marketplace.

An autonomous business model often develops when a company is reacting to a major change, such as new and disruptive technology (described in greater detail in Chapter Eight). Creating a new organization that is not bound by the old business model may be the only way to compete in a new marketplace. Sprint PCS is such a case. To take advantage of the burgeoning cellular phone market, Sprint created a new organization with an autonomous business model rather than a new sales channel within the existing organization.

Business Models in the Environment

Each organization's business model(s) compete in the environment with business models from other companies. Opportunities in the market-place and obstacles created by competitors all factor into the effective-ness of each business model.

Another way to describe a company's business model is to compare and contrast it to other business models in the environment. This often leads to insights about how to make improvements, react to competi-tion, and develop new strategies.

There are four basic types of business models in the environment:

1. Competitive
2. Substitutable
3. Complementary
4. Parallel

A *competitive business model* sells a similar product or service into the same market space. They represent "the direct competition." For ex-ample, the Honda Accord competes directly with the Toyota Camry, McDonald's competes directly with Wendy's, and United Airlines com-petes directly with American Airlines. However, this definition often can be too narrow for strategic purposes. Consumers may chose to buy a truck instead of a Honda Accord, eat at home instead of at McDon-ald's, or drive on their next vacation instead of flying.

Substitutable business models represent the choices buyers can make by meeting their needs with products or services from different cate-gories. For example, cars and trucks are, for the most part, substitutable. Fast-food restaurants compete with restaurants in general, and grocery stores, too. Airlines compete in a general transportation marketplace with trains, busses, and even cars.

Substitutable business models are often ignored, but can represent the greatest long-term threat. Entire markets can disappear as customers switch to substitutable products or services. Computers and adding machines were once in separate market spaces. Now computers have virtually made adding machines obsolete.

Complementary business models represent products or services that are normally bought or used together, even though different companies may sell them. For example, oil and oil filters, hammers and nails, hardware and software are used together, and often purchased together, but typically made by different companies.

Microsoft has grown partly by incorporating the software features provided by companies with complementary business models into its own products. Often, adding complementary products or services is seen as a logical path for growth.

Parallel business models represent products or services that don't compete for the same customers, but may share similar technologies or have similar acquisition and sales channels. For example, Caterpillar Truck Engines and Lycoming Aircraft Engines don't compete for customers, but they do employ similar technologies and sell their products through channels that employ similar methodologies.

Often good ideas can be gleaned from parallel business models. For example, if an improved method for manufacturing pistons is put in place by Lycoming for aircraft engines, the same technology may filter into Caterpillar truck engines.

Companies do not have to share business models to be competitors. A retailer can compete with a cataloger, a farmer-owned wholesale co-op can compete with a publicly-owned wholesaler that buys on the open market, an Internet company can compete with a bricks-and-mortar company.

Creating and Competing with Business Models

Most business models start out as simply outright copies of other successful business models or revisions of an existing model. All the basic rules of business must apply, whether a new business model uses new or old buying and selling channels and a new or old value-added process.

With any business model, it should be clear what makes the value-added process competitive and how the company can earn a return on investment (ROI).

The real trick in creating a new business model is not just knowing what to copy, but rather it is knowing from where new threats may arise. In order to determine how to organize to compete with other companies' business models, it is first necessary to determine what each company's current business model is. Then, do a SWOT analysis (Strengths, Weaknesses, Opportunities, and Threats) for that business model that includes a comparison to other business models in the environment.

For competitive business models, several key distinctions that should be considered are:

- Acquisition methodology
- Cost structure
- Delivery channels

For example, one company may control the manufacturing of a product and emphasize quality, while another imports from foreign manufacturers and emphasizes low cost. One company may use retail stores, while another sells through mail-order catalogs. Each may be reaching the same audience with roughly similar products.

For substitutable business models, several key distinctions that should be considered are:

- Overlapping product capabilities
- End-user usage cost
- How customers use the product or service

In reviewing substitutable products, be keenly aware of products that have growing or changing capabilities and falling cost structures. Examples of areas where this has been a major factor are cars or sport utility vehicles, film or digital cameras, and CDs or DVDs. If the substitutable offer is a disruptive technology, it may replace the original product entirely, e.g., DVDs have all but replaced VHS videos in the movie and television show rental market.

For parallel business models, several key distinctions that should be considered are:

- Adaptability of technology/methodology
- Cost structure
- Customer usage

The idea with looking at parallel business models is to try to "steal smart" and come up with different, and somewhat proven, ways to give customers a more useful product and/or to lower costs. Often, both technology and organizational structures can be adapted. Pay particular attention to technology that requires a different organizational structure to be marketed successfully, as that is where both the greatest challenges and greatest opportunities can be found.

For autonomous business models, key considerations are:

- Whether or not a division should be spun-off or sold
- If capital and management considerations are being spent on the right business models
- What opportunities for "cross-pollination" exist among the different business models in terms of technology, methodology, and human skills

Managing autonomous business models can be a very complex management question. However, it is clear to see that changes to the business model(s) at this level must be understood at the top, and being a part of a conglomerate can greatly alter a division's ability to manage change.

Understanding the Internal Culture

In order to properly understand any business model, one should first understand three of the main forces driving and determining the internal culture of a company:

1. The UVP
2. The Organization Chart
3. The Information Systems

The unique value proposition (UVP) is a basic picture of what the company does and what sets it apart from competitors. (The UVP is described in greater detail below.)

The organization chart reflects the organization's strategy (or what the strategy was when the chart was created) and represents the formal chain-of-command.

The information systems structure typically represents islands of data and knowledge. The systems were designed at some point in the past to support tactics and strategy (mostly tactics) as it was seen then, around departments or functional areas as they existed. What is important to realize is that people tend to work with people using the same systems and become isolated from people using other systems. This becomes a challenge for both technology and human interaction.

Before attempting to build a team to revamp the business model, the first steps for top management in working with the internal culture are to describe the UVP, organization chart, and the basic information systems structure. Then, review it with other managers and advisors who are honest enough to give unbiased feedback. It is necessary that top management clearly defines where the organization is at now so that a business modeling team has a place to begin when determining where the organization should go.

Describing the Unique Value Proposition (UVP)

The *unique value proposition (UVP)* is what differentiates the organization's business model from that of other organizations competing to serve the same or similar customer needs.

It is important not to confuse the UVP with the mission statement. A *mission statement* should focus on goals, beliefs, and core competencies. Even in the case of true commodity products, merely noting things like "quality," "service," and "value" is not sufficient to distinguish one UVP from another. However, such key words often bulk up mission statements.

The UVP is the "hook" that, ideally, makes the organization indispensable to their customers. It often is reflected in the *unique selling proposition (the USP)* that, like the UVP is the one single, special reason that an individual becomes and stays a customer. For example, it is the reason that Neiman Marcus customers continue to buy at their stores even though there are good, lower-cost substitutes. And, conversely, it is the single reason that Wal-Mart shoppers stay loyal to Wal-Mart, despite the lack of "ambiance." Competing companies can have very similar mission statements, but it is ideal to have a distinctly different UVP from competitors. Knowing that the UVP is not like the mission statement helps make defining it in a simple, direct fashion much easier.

Business models can be similar in structure, but different in operation due to their differing UVPs. For example, retailers often compete with different UVPs. Some retailers rely on being in high-traffic locations. Others prefer low-overhead locations that allow them to sell for less or offer more selection in a larger store. Both seek to offer customers greater value or convenience, but in a different way.

Innovation can be part of the UVP and can be compared among organizations. An organization that is innovating successfully will have a high share of its sales and profits coming from new products, patented items, and so on.

Expertise for professional organizations, unique production

capabilities for manufacturers, and local or regional specialization for all kinds of organizations can all be legitimate components of the UVP.

Information Flow Within the Business Model

The business model is divided into acquisition, processing and/or distribution, and sales, which is quite often reflective of both systems and organizational culture. It is important to understand and be able to describe in basic terms what each department does, as each department's system will invariably be designed to support those functions.

The point of describing the information flow is to determine where detail and accuracy have been demanded and where they have not. For example, purchasing departments will have detailed and accurate information regarding the cost of raw materials. However, the sales department may not have such information. Sales is more likely to have detailed, accurate data about who bought what, for how much, and when, but will most likely have to rely on other departments for cost-of-goods sold data.

Cross-silo information flow, or the lack of it, is important to understand. Most people are surprised to find their most cherished assumptions made about data from other departments are often false.

Defining Which Behaviors Can Be Measured

Behavior can best be tracked where action takes place and accurate information describing the actions is stored. The amount of goods shipped can best be tracked using data from the system supporting distribution. The quantity of new items acquired can best be tracked using data from receiving. The cost of a new item acquired can best be tracked using data from purchasing.

Initially, it may be impossible to accurately determine some data points. For example, a manufacturer levies the cost-of-goods sold percentage by manufacturing plant, based on the total cost of operating each plant and the total sales of each plant. The cost-of-goods sold percentage is updated by plant annually.

In this case, it could not be determined if one product line produced in a given plant is more profitable than another product line produced in the same plant. They could be selling one product for a loss and another at a profit, without anyone being able to be sure.

In a case where cost-of-goods was deemed inaccurate, simply using revenue to determine how successful one product line is compared to another, or how valuable one customer is compared to another, may have to suffice, at least temporarily.

What people bought, when they bought, and in what combinations they bought defines their value to the organization and defines the success of the business model. As a result, the heart-and-soul of the information system is the transactional database. Ultimately, the transaction is *the point* at which the organization's stimuli meet the customer's response. Measuring behavior, at the point of transaction, is the single most important data set for any business modeling effort.

Demographics, focus groups, and survey research have a place, but transactional data will always be the most valuable component of the database. But any data-driven business modeling effort has, at its core, the corporate knowledge and experience built at the point of transaction. Before commissioning a market study, before creating a new survey, and before analyzing demographics, managers need a clear understanding of who their best customers are, how many customers make up 80 percent of their sales, and how many customers are actually served at a profit.

Transactional data are factual and behavior-based. Behavioral predictions made using transaction-based behavioral data tend to correlate extremely well with future behavior. Building around transactional data as the core set of facts in a business modeling effort is the key to success.

Describing the Customers

Most business models that fail do so because of a misunderstanding of the customer base. Often managers are unable to correctly define their customer segments. Which group is responsible for the bulk of the company's sales? Who are the profitable repeat customers? Who are the marginally profitable prospects? Properly understanding the customer base well enough to create an accurate description is essential to developing a sound business model.

For example, one company sold gardening equipment to both the business and consumer markets. The company was marginally profitable and thought that to grow their business they needed to target their consumer market since there are millions of consumer prospects and only thousands of lawn-care related businesses. Initially, they began prospecting for consumers using the same financial goals that they had used for the business market. Soon, it became apparent that their prospecting efforts were ineffective.

To determine why, the company analyzed their data and discovered that their business market was quite a bit more valuable than their consumer market. They re-couped their advertising expenditures when a typical business became a customer. When a typical consumer became a customer, they did not re-coup their advertising expenditures. Each segment of their market had to be targeted with different financial goals.

Acting upon the information from their analysis, the company developed specific goals and strategies for reaching both segments of their market. The results were dramatic. Within a year this near break-even company was making a major profit.

How do companies learn more about their markets? There are several methods for describing markets and analyzing the unique features of each segment. Before discussing these methods in depth, let's define some terms so that we have a common understanding upon which to build our discussion.

We'll start by describing the most basic view of an organization's marketplace. Consider the following graphic, which describes this most basic view:

Exhibit 2.1: Marketplace Segments

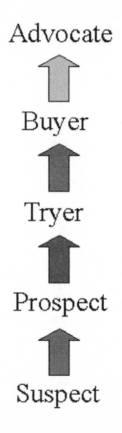

Let's start with Suspect. *Suspects* are people or organizations who are in the general marketplace of potential customers but who are not specifically identified. For example, everyone who reads the local newspaper is a suspect for a sporting goods store. The sporting goods store doesn't know exactly who reads their local paper, but they know their readers live in the same area where their stores are located. While the store's owners think many of the newspaper readers will be interested in and able to buy their sporting goods, they have not yet targeted any of these readers for specific contact.

Prospects (prospective customers) are people or organizations that have been specifically identified as potential customers. They may have been selected from the marketplace of suspects, or they may have identified themselves as prospects. For example, the sporting goods store may target parents of children ages six through twelve because they know these children are likely to be involved in intramural sports. The store would certainly consider people who came to the store and inquired about team sportswear to be prospects, particularly if they coached a team. The store likely would keep a list of local coaches, league officials, and so on. A suspect who saw an ad in the paper would become a prospect once they entered the store, called for information, or requested information to be sent to them online.

Tryers are people or organizations that have made one or only a few minor purchases. Typically, tryers are one-time buyers, but they may have made a few smaller "test" purchases. For example, a parent coming into the sporting goods store for the first time and buying an outfit for their child who is playing on her first softball team is a tryer. A new customer buying hiking boots for their vacation is also a tryer. A prospect becomes a tryer when he makes his first purchase.

Buyers are people or organizations that have made several purchases, but who cannot yet be considered loyal customers. In other words, they have not yet demonstrated a consistent buying pattern. A parent who has come into the sporting goods store every year for three years to equip their child with the team-selected softball gear, but doesn't come in at other times of the year is a buyer. Someone who became a tryer last week and came back for a second purchase today is also a buyer. A tryer becomes a buyer when he makes a second purchase or demonstrates an inconsistent repeat purchase pattern.

Advocates are people or organizations who have made many purchases and who are very likely to continue to make many purchases. A parent of three children, each of whom plays multiple sports, and who typically spends several hundred dollars a month at the store is an advocate. Someone who coaches several teams, buys their team equipment at the store, and selects uniforms for team members to buy at the store is also an advocate. A buyer becomes an advocate when he makes multiple purchases and demonstrates a consistent pattern of buying.

As a rule, nearly all profits come from advocates. They are the 10 percent or 20 percent of customers that provide 80 percent or 90 percent of all sales. Usually the most efficient way to gain more advocates is to find ways to convert more buyers into advocates. Buyers are marginally profitable to market to, especially if they have bought recently.

Most organizations actually lose money converting suspects and prospects into tryers. Generally, organizations spend more money on advertising and marketing to create new customers than they earn on the first sale to new customers, or "tryers." It is only through repeat sales and buyers moving up the tryer-buyer-advocate hierarchy that most organizations can make and then maximize profit.

Knowing that we spend more money on advertising to create new customers than we earn through initial sales to those customers leads us to the concept of *lifetime value*. Broadly, lifetime value is today's value of likely future sales to customers, minus the costs of serving and communicating with those customers.

For example, the parent of one 16-year-old child who plays only one sport probably has a very low lifetime value. The parent of a five-year-old and a seven-year-old who coaches different teams for each child, probably has a very high lifetime value. A wise sporting goods store manager would be willing to spend much more of his advertising dollars to attract the second parent into his store.

Segmentation is a generic term that describes any way marketers may divide the marketplace in order to reach different groups or targets with different messages. Most segmentation is more complex than suspect-prospect-tryer-buyer-advocate, but nearly all organizations can, in some simple fashion, fit their segments within those descriptors.

With the example of the sporting goods store, segmentation may result in a basic communication plan like the following:

- Suspects: Newspaper and radio advertising
- Prospects: Email newsletters (if requested), in-store displays, mailed newsletter for officials and coaches, plus suspect communication
- Tryers: Coupons at checkout, offer to sign up for free newsletter, plus prospect communication
- Buyers: Mail or email seasonal specials, specials on purchases over $100, plus tryer communication
- Advocates: Free seasonal sports clinics, new product samples, free gear for coaches with team purchase, plus buyer communication

As you can imagine, a sporting goods store that followed a basic segmentation like the one just described would have a substantial advantage over a store that treated everyone the same.

Cross-tabulation analysis (or cross-tab analysis) is a basic way of comparing any two variables. It is a good place to start when trying to describe relationships using data. Comparing different "market" variables such as age, income, or family size against "response" variables such as average order or average annual spending, reveals basic relationships that may be sufficient to support your strategy. For example, consider two sample charts that are part of a cross-tab analysis for a sporting goods store in Exhibits 2.2 and 2.3.

Exhibit 2.2: Cross-Tab Analysis: Spending and Number of Children

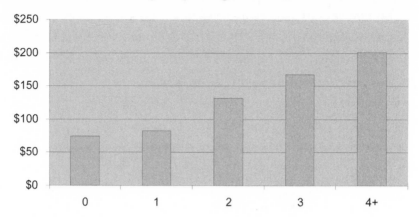

Clearly, more kids equals more sports equipment.

Looking at Exhibit 2.3, we can see that older parents generally spend more, but a parent of two children (regardless of age) probably spends more than an older parent of one child. We can't know that for sure by cross-tab analysis alone, but we can infer it may be likely. As a general rule, things that appear to be important in a cross-tab analysis tend to be important in multi-variable analyses, and things that appear not to be important in a cross-tab analysis are usually not important in multi-variable analyses as well. Cross-tab analysis is a good place to begin our

Exhibit 2.3: Cross-Tab Analysis: Spending and Age of Parent

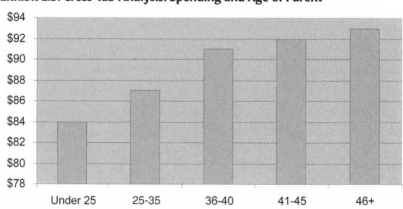

marketplace assessment since it gives us a solid understand of which simple relationships are meaningful and which are not, before we move on to analyze our more complex sets of relationships.

Profiling

Profiling is a data-driven process intended to create an overall description of customers and/or prospects. Profiling identifies and defines basic characteristics of buyers and/or prospects.

Through combining demographics (age, income, marital status, etc.) and psychographics (hobbies, lifestyle, product, service and brand preferences) the profiling process will enable you to describe the predominant demographic/lifestyle characteristics of your current customers.

Profiling is based primarily on simple cross-tabulations, such as sales versus buyer type. By looking at a variety of relatively simple associations, one after the other, it is possible to develop a simple picture of the characteristics, behaviors, and results that correlate most highly. Customers can be profiled along just about any dimension using this tool: age, income, and number of purchases, for example. Sometimes, a simple comparison to some "outside" data, such as a national average, is included. The results can be presented as a table, but often are shown as a "histogram" like the one in Exhibit 2.4.

Profiling is generally a good place to start any analysis; it is relatively

Exhibit 2.4: Customer Profile Histogram

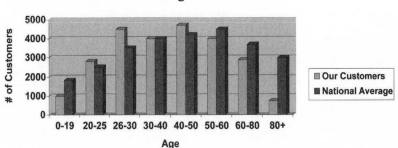

easy and inexpensive to do and can be very helpful in either business-to-business or business-to-consumer marketing. Profiling is the preferred method for an enterprise to use to determine the answers to such questions as:

- What do current customers and prospects "look like"?
- How diverse are current buyers and prospects?
- What are their socio-economic descriptors?
- Which hobbies, activities, and interests are most appealing to them?
- What family and life-cycle stages are they typically in?
- Where are they located?
- What is the current market penetration by profile (demographic and lifestyle)?
- What are the best ways to describe the overall customer base?

Simple profiling is limited to assessing customers in only one or two ways or dimensions at a time. When looking at different groups of customers and comparing them in three or more ways simultaneously, the tables and graphs quickly become quite complicated and confusing.

The key disadvantage of profiling is that it assesses the customer or patron base as a whole, and not by customer segments. If profitable customers are atypical, and unprofitable customers comprise the majority of the house file, the profile will depict mainly unprofitable customers. Descriptive and predictive modeling (discussed later in this chapter) can describe these differing segments that profiling will miss.

Profiling is typically used when basic knowledge about the customers or prospects will directly affect how they are targeted. Profiling offers a description of customers that marketers can use to create appropriate offers or messages.

Information that might be found in a profile includes such items as:

Exhibit 2.5: Smart Household Cluster Descriptions

SMART HOUSEHOLD CLUSTER DESCRIPTIONS

SMART HOUSEHOLD CLUSTER A09

Rank	1	Household Cluster		Family Cluster
U.S. Household Count:		503,941		11,520,153
U.S. Household Percent:		0.58		11.37
U.S. Household Rank:		72 of 144		5 of 15

DEMOGRAPHICS	Cluster	National	Index	Strength
Averages:				
Head of Household Age	46.0	46.9	98	(0)
Length of Residence	9.0	7.2	125	(+)
Home Value	$52,815	$113,677	46	(-)(-)
Household Size	6.10	1.92	317	(+)(+)
Household Income ($K)	$35	$53	66	(-)
Medians:				
Net Worth ($K)	$36	$39	92	(-)
Age of Structure	31	27	115	(+)
Percents:				
Female Householder	1.92%	30.15%	6	(-)(-)
Married Householder	96.40%	35.04%	275	(+)(+)
Children in Household	91.01%	38.97%	234	(+)(+)
Homeowner	87.73%	61.20%	143	(+)
White Collar	41.77%	53.53%	78	(-)(-)
Geographic:				
Urban Rural Ratio	3.81	3.03	126	(0)
Population Density/Sq. Mile	1,064	6,865	16	(-)

DEMOGRAPHIC TRAITS	Strength
Number of Adults per Household	(+)(+)
Number of Children per Household	(+)(+)
Children - Age 4 to 6	(+)(+)
Children - Age 13 to 18	(+)(+)
Children - Age 7 to 9	(+)(+)
Max Education Level - High School	(+)(+)
Occupation - Agricultural	(+)(+)
Occupation - Machine Operators, Assemblers	(+)(+)
Occupation - Transportation, Material Moving	(+)(+)
Travel Time to Work	(-)(-)

HEAD OF HOUSEHOLD AGE DISTRIBUTION

Cluster Pct / National Pct

1	18-24
2	25-34
3	35-44
4	45-54
5	55-64
6	65-74
7	75+

HOUSEHOLD INCOME DISTRIBUTION

Cluster Pct / National Pct

1	<$15K
2	$15K-$25K
3	$25K-$35K
4	$35K-$50K
5	$50K-$75K
6	$75K-$100K
7	$100K-$150K
8	$150K+

STRONG LIFESTYLE TRAITS

- Bought car or truck tires in the last year
- Heavy/frequent grocery shopper
- Own or lease any domestic auto
- Own or lease any van, truck, or SUV
- Bought kitchen appliances
- Own workshop equipment
- Collector
- Own a VCR or camcorder
- Dog or cat owner
- Drinks any type of non-alcoholic beverages

WEAK LIFESTYLE TRAITS

- Drinks any type of wine
- Use convenience banking products or services
- Rent any vehicle
- Drinks any type of distilled spirits
- Has any credit card
- Shopped at home electronics store in last 3 months
- Investor
- Own or lease any foreign auto
- Shopped at office supply/computer store in last 3 m
- Strong political opinions

SUMMARIZED CREDIT TRAITS

	Strength
Credit Inquiries - Past 12 Months	(-)(-)
Service/Professional Trades	(-)(-)
Service/Professional Trades - Loan Amount	(-)(-)
Bank Card Trades - Balance/Loan Ratio	(-)(-)
Balance on All Trades	(-)(-)
All Trades - Opened Past 12 Months	(-)(-)
All Trades - Opened Past 36 Months	(-)(-)
Bank Trades - 30+ Days Delinquent	(+)(+)
CU Trades - Loan Amount	(-)(-)
Open Credit Union Trades	(-)(-)
All Trades - Balance/Loan Ratio	(-)(-)
Real Property Trades - Loan Amount	(-)(-)

Relative to National Average: (+)(+) = Much Greater Than; (+) = Greater Than; (0) = Little Difference; (-) = Less Than; (-)(-) = Much Less Than.
Cooperatively Developed by Ruf Strategic Solutions and Experian.

Please See Household Cluster Descriptions Tab for National Averages and Other Detail.
Smart Household Cluster Descriptions - Page 1

- The average age for customers is 49.
- Eighty-three percent of customers own their own home.
- Sixty percent of customers have made only one purchase.
- Eighty percent of purchases are below the average order amount.
- Males have an average order of $85.00, while females have an average order of $62.00.

Profiling can be a highly effective tool for marketers who want to gain a better understanding of a complex customer/prospect database. Exhibit 2.5 is an example of a profile that includes distribution of age and income compared to national averages, along with demographics and lifestyle traits that are significantly above or below national averages.

Mapping as a Profiling Tool

Mapping is an excellent profiling tool, but be careful. A national map that shows customer counts that are high in high population density areas, like New York and Los Angeles, doesn't really provide you with much useful information. But, a map that shows you where your customers are located and whose variations can be logically accounted for is very helpful. Consider the map in Exhibit 2.6 showing customers by U.S. postal region. The customer base for this company is strong relative to population in the South and in the Sunbelt, but not as strong in the high population areas of the Northeast and upper Midwest.

Profit-Based Segmentation

The basic characteristics identified through profiling can be enhanced by creating a *profit-based segmentation*. Profiling is often done in conjunction with profit-based segmentation.

Questions that profit-based segmentation should answer include:

- Who are the best customers?
- What is the lifetime value of customer segments?

Sample Company
Trade Area Analysis by ZIP3

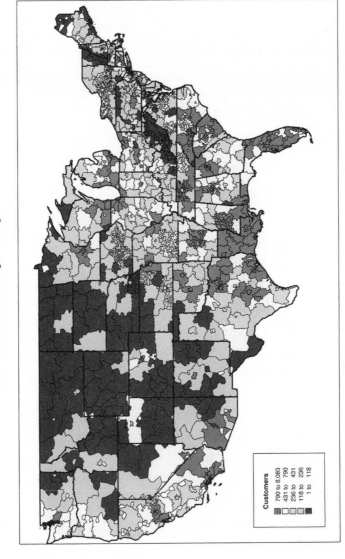

Customers
- 790 to 8,083
- 431 to 790
- 236 to 431
- 118 to 236
- 1 to 118

Developed by Ruf Strategic Solutions

Courtesy of Kurt Ruf, RUF Strategic Solutions. Reproduced with permission.

- How many tryers, buyers, and advocates are there? (Good, better, best?)
- Are different products purchased by different kinds of buyers?
- Which sources, offers, media, and sales channels bring which kinds of customers? Which have the best customer retention?
- Which customers should be contacted more often and which should be contacted less often or not at all?
- Compared to working on customer retention, is the organization emphasizing customer acquisition too much or not enough?

A variety of analyses are used to create profit-based segmentation. These include:

- *Pareto's Rule* (Eighty percent of sales or profits are generated by 20 percent of the customer base.)—determining if the bulk of sales or profits (the 80 percent) comes from a minority of customers (the 20 percent), and determining who those "best customers" are.
- *RFM* or *RFA*—building a hierarchy of customers based on *R*ecency (how long ago they purchased), *F*requency (how many times they purchased), and *M*onetary (how much they spent in total). For most organizations, *A* (Average Order) can be used in place of *M*onetary, as it tends to be a better predictor of future behavior.
- *RFM/P*—*P* stands for *P*roduct (what customers bought) or *P*rofitability. Often customers are segmented by category of item they buy, or by profit margin of items they buy.
- *LTV*—Lifetime value is often used to determine different buyer segments by type (business vs. consumer) or source (direct mail vs. retail) and indicates whether prospecting efforts are in balance with retention efforts.

- *House File Inventory*—The House File Inventory analysis shows how many customers are in which segments. It is a key component to building a successful marketing strategy.

Profit-based segmentation is often done before using the techniques of predictive or descriptive modeling (which will be discussed in the next section) for three reasons. Profit-based segmentation:

1. Can normally be accomplished with data that have already been captured by most organizations
2. Greatly improves the accuracy and effectiveness of more advanced analytical techniques by providing an understanding of who the tryer, buyer, and advocate customers are
3. Is typically an adequate stand-alone technique for mining the customer base

What can profit-based segmentation tell a company? An agricultural company whose target market was farmers who worked 500 acres or more used profit-based segmentation to analyze their promotional sales database. To their surprise, they learned that the majority of people they were tracking in this database weren't customers. The free hats and jackets were not being given away to their big buyers. Instead the company had been tracking and marketing to less than 10 percent of their target market. Using profit-based segmentation helped this company realize that their promotional sales were missing the customer segment that purchased more than 80 percent of their product.

Sometimes, relationships are so complex that profiling and profit-based segmentation are not adequate to describe what is going on. Nevertheless, these basic techniques are the place to start before moving on to other modeling methodologies.

Predictive Modeling

Predictive modeling is a methodology that utilizes the individual characteristics (behaviors) that correlate with the purchase behavior of customers. This methodology then correlates customer behavior and lifestyle factors to their propensity to buy a product or service.

The findings of the predictive modeling process are driven by data, not by opinion or any other biases, except, perhaps, bad data. Typically, the results can be used to consistently predict future prospect behavior. Using predictive modeling techniques, it is possible to limit target selection to only those most likely to buy or to place a substantial order.

Predictive modeling is the preferred method for an enterprise to use to help them determine the answers to such questions as:

- Who are the best targets for my promotions?
- How many prospects exist that look like (will act like) my best customers?
- Which existing "smaller" buyers are most likely to become "bigger" buyers?
- Which prospects are most likely to respond?
- Which prospects are most likely to buy?
- If they buy, how much will/can they spend?

In order for predictive modeling to be effective, it is important to first understand customer-buying patterns. The model must rely on accurate response, sales, and margin data to maximize effectiveness. Building accurate RFM or RFA and knowledge prior to creating a predictive model will assure better results.

Predictive modeling can be based on a variety of techniques, including regression analysis, CHAID (Chi-Square Automatic Interaction Detector), and C&RT (Classification and Regression Tree), to name a few. Techniques such as regression analysis apply a score reflecting the predicted likelihood or degree to each record, whereas CHAID and C&RT

segment each record into mutually exclusive segments. These techniques are discussed in detail in Chapter Five.

In many cases, such as when using CHAID or C&RT, the prediction is based on sales per target or the expected average sale divided by the expected average order. This is a simple means of selecting the best customers or prospects with one predictive model.

Predictive modeling is most effective when used to select the best names from a list (or to de-select the worst names). Predictive modeling is typically less effective than profiling when it is used to describe the attributes of customers and prospects. It is typically of less value than profiling or descriptive modeling for building knowledge to create targeted offers.

When would a company use predictive modeling? One organization created a predictive model after they had done profit-based segmentation. The company wanted to better understand why they had a high attrition rate and what they could do to improve their customer retention rates. They had already determined that attrition dropped among companies that had made four or more purchases in a year. However, from this group, the company still lost a substantial portion each year. Predictive modeling helped them find a segment that bought four or more times, in four or more product categories, and had two or more contacts at the same location that had an attrition rate of zero. Predictive modeling found the combination of variables that equated to low or no attrition.

Armed with the knowledge from the predictive modeling technique, the company reviewed their situation. They found they had accounts spending over $1 million a year, but they only had one contact name. So, they built a strategy to develop a second contact among companies with only one current contact. They found they had large accounts buying only one item, so they targeted companies buying one or only a few types of products, and created special offers for them if they would buy additional types of products. The predictive modeling results took what was a very complex situation and made it simpler to manage. They could quickly review each account, and determine which offers they should make to improve their chances of keeping that account.

A major U.S. symphony used predictive modeling to dramatically improve subscription marketing effectiveness. The improvements amounted to approximately $500,000 dollars a year in either increased revenue or decreased costs compared to the "industry standard" approach they had been using just two years prior. Marketing campaigns now are dramatically smaller and less expensive, with a similar overall revenue result compared to larger and more expensive campaigns.

In short, improved knowledge from better use of the database resulted in the following changes:

1. Instead of one very large new-buyer acquisition campaign that marginally broke even or had a loss, the symphony now conducts a series of smaller, profitable campaigns.
2. Marketers can identify and reach prospects they could not previously identify. The process can find a handful of good prospects from a poorly performing list that would otherwise be ignored.
3. Demographic and psychographic names have been virtually eliminated in favor of lists based on behavior gathered through list trades.

Descriptive Modeling

The objective of *descriptive modeling* is to find and describe distinct groups in the customer/prospect database. The knowledge helps in understanding customers beyond an overall average. It helps to create relevant offers to each customer segment. With this knowledge, communication with customers can be more effective because it is based on their needs and characteristics.

Customers tend to be in multiple segments based on demographics (income level, age, ethnic, number of children, lifestyle, etc.). Most

companies know the overall averages of their customers' demographics; unfortunately these averages don't describe the differences among
customers. For example, the average customer earns $50,000, but
there might be a group of customers who earn more than $90,000, and
another group of customers who earn less than $25,000. The needs of
these two groups are probably different than those with $50,000
incomes.

There are two basic approaches to descriptive modeling. Both are
based upon a descriptive statistical technique called "cluster analysis,"
but one uses generalized clusters that are pre-defined, the other creates
custom clusters to match the specific data being modeled.

The first approach is called a *static cluster analysis*. A static cluster is
defined *in advance* as a collection of many characteristics that are ob-
served to "go together" as a group. One popular list service (Prizm™)
has defined 62 static clusters based upon average income, average age,
average number of children, and so forth. They assign every neighborhood in the United States to one of these 62 pre-defined clusters on the
basis of Zip Code, census block group, and data about the households of
immediate neighbors.

Each static cluster has a list of attributes and a name such as "Money
& Brains" or "Upward Bound." The underlying assumption is that if
your customer lives in the neighborhood that is assigned to a specific
cluster, then on average your customer is like all others in the cluster,
and that the average description of the cluster accurately describes your
customer, too. Sometimes this is true. More often, it is not.

The advantages of a static cluster analysis are that it can be done relatively quickly, requires little work on the part of the organization that is
buying the analysis (other than providing a list of names and addresses
to be modeled), and that the prospect lists that can be rented match clusters that occur most frequently in the customer file.

The disadvantages of a static cluster analysis are that it doesn't describe best customers (or relate to profitability or sales), it is not designed as a "predictive model" (so, it is not the most effective technique

to determine who will buy), and it is not uniquely fitted to data of any specific organization.

The second approach is called a *dynamic cluster analysis.* A dynamic cluster is defined only *after* statistically analyzing each specific organization's data. The analysis process assembles customers into clusters based upon their specific demographic, lifestyle, and psychographic characteristics at a household—not a Zip Code or neighborhood—level of detail. Since dynamic clusters are defined only by the organization's customers, the clusters tend to be much more precise, descriptive, and useful.

Dynamic cluster analysis usually reveals that a company's customers can be accurately described with only a few clusters, i.e., five or six, rather than dozens. This greatly simplifies the job of selecting the media and message most appropriate for your specific needs.

Dynamic clustering is the preferred method to determine the answers to the following questions:

- Who are my current customers and prospects?
- How demographically diverse are the current buyer and prospect groups?
- What is the socio-economic profile of each buyer or prospect group at the household level?
- Which hobbies, activities, and interests are most appealing to each group?
- What family and life-cycle stage is each group in?
- What are the best ways to describe each buyer or prospect group?

Whether using a dynamic or a static cluster analysis, marketers often refer to results as "mood music for copywriters," since it is considered by some to be more useful for providing a feel for customers than it is for selecting customers to contact.

It should be noted that the same statistical technique that drives a cluster analysis is typically used to group opinion survey respondents. Responders with similar answers can be grouped in the same way consumers with similar demographics and lifestyles can be grouped.

The following is a brief example of descriptive analysis. It is based on an alumni organization that wanted to know if their product and service offers were relevant to their members and potential members. The technique used is cluster analysis.

Among other things, cluster analysis told the alumni organization how many natural groups there are in their database, the average income for each group, ownership of house, and so forth. The process found the natural grouping, described each group, and highlighted the major differences between each group.

Cluster analysis helped the organization to understand how alumni are different and how to package offers to meet different needs. Cluster analysis was also useful in dividing the alumni into groups to target with different media. With cluster analysis the alumni board was better equipped to build better relationships with members by knowing who the members are and what the members need.

Some of the different groups discovered in the alumni organization's database were labeled as follows:

- Old Comrades
- College Joe
- Golfing at the Club
- Cocooning Tech
- Eternal Student

A descriptive analysis of each group was developed and is detailed in Exhibit 2.7. Using this analysis, the alumni organization was able to provide more focused services for their members and to develop more targeted fund-raising appeals.

Exhibit 2.7: Groups in the Alumni Organization's Database

Cocooning Techies are about 16.5% of the alumni.

1) Average income is about $63,000/year
2) Average age: 42.55
3) Average number of kids: 1.55
4) 69% in Missouri
5) Enjoy CDs, Cable TV, Stereo Buff, Sports on TV, PCs
6) Do not enjoy Hunting/Shooting, RVs, Automotive Work, Motorcycling, Stamp/Coin Collecting

This group is younger and slight above average in income. What kind of approach will attract their attention; money-saving offers, improve social status offers?

Eternal Students are about 11.31% of the alumni.

1) Average income is about $16,000/year
2) Average age: 41.43
3) Average number of kids: 1.00
4) 67.42% in Missouri
5) Enjoy Stereo Buff, CDs, Exercise, Cultural/Arts, Cable TV
6) Do not enjoy Hunting/Shooting, RVs, Automotive Work, Fishing, Sewing

This group is younger and below average in income. Are they likely to respond to money-saving offers?

Old Comrades are about 7.78% of the alumni.

1) Average income is about $41,000/year
2) Average age: 70
3) Average number of kids: < 1
4) 66% in Missouri
5) Enjoy Cable TV, Travel in USA, Book Reading, TV Sports, Records/CDs
6) Do not enjoy Hunting/Shooting, RVs, Automotive Work, Motorcycling, Video Games

This group is older and average in income; they enjoy reading and traveling. This segment is small relative to other segments.

(Continued)

Exhibit 2.7: Groups in the Alumni Organization's Database (Continued)

Golfing at the Club are about 20% of the alumni.

1) Average income is about $125,000/year
2) Average age: 47.86
3) Average number of kids: 1.45
4) 61% in Missouri
5) Enjoys CDs, PCs, Exercise, Golf, Investing
6) Does not enjoy Hunting/Shooting, RVs, Automotive Work, Motorcycling, Sweepstakes

This is an affluent group. What service/activities can we offer them?

College Joes are about 16% of the alumni.

1) Average income is about $90,000/year
2) Average age: 48
3) Average number of kids: 1.4
4) 71% in Missouri
5) Enjoy CDs, PCs, Exercise, Golf, Travel in USA
6) Do not enjoy Hunting/Shooting, RVs, Automotive Work, Motorcycling, Stamp/Coin Collecting

What activities/services would this group be interested in? A 10% discount for golf club membership?

Multi-Channel Profiling

Multi-channel profiling is one of several descriptive segmenting techniques used to identify the types of customers brought into the company by various traceable marketing channels or sources, such as retail stores, catalogs, and websites. After segmenting the customers by channels, the analysis then determines the inherent profitability of each of the customers both within and across each channel. The knowledge gained from a multi-channel performance analysis allows a company to drive customers to the channel most likely to maximize profits.

Multi-channel profiling is most necessary when customers that buy through different means are tracked differently. For example, if Web buyers are not matched against store buyers or catalog buyers, it is not possible to tell if they are buying in one or several places. Perhaps Web buyers are only Web buyers and store buyers are only store buyers. Or, perhaps the best customers tend to buy from both outlets. Multi-channel profiling helps determine how much cross-channel selling goes on, whether it corresponds to more sales or merely cannibalizes sales, and which channels tend to produce new customers with the best chance of becoming advocates.

To conduct a multi-channel performance analysis, organizations obviously must have the ability to capture names and addresses of customers or patrons through multiple channels (websites, print ads, TV, direct mail, sweepstakes, etc.). If, in addition, an organization is also able to capture information about their customers' behavior (what they bought, when, and for how much), multi-channel profiling can be a *very* powerful strategic tool.

Multi-channel profiling starts with analyzing the names and addresses of an organization's current customers or patrons and the channel through which the customer enters the organization's house file. The "house file" is the database of customer and prospect names owned by the organization. Differences are highlighted among customers in terms of profitability and, in some cases, demographic profile. The information that is gleaned helps organizations communicate with their customers by using different channels to maximize their entire marketing program's return on investment (ROI).

Usually the ROI performance differs from channel to channel. One channel may offer a low cost for attracting prospects, but turn few prospects into customers. Another channel may find few prospects, but have high repeat business among customers.

A variety of tools and research techniques can be included to describe the predominant demographic/lifestyle picture of customers and prospects by channel. Information about the actual households or businesses assists in answering the following questions about the customers from each channel:

- Who are these current customers?
- What is their socio-economic profile?
- Where is their physical location?
- What is the current market penetration by geographic area and profile (demographic and lifestyle)?
- Where is market penetration the highest?

Specific to each channel, it is possible to develop knowledge to answer the following questions:

- Are the profiles of Web customers significantly different compared to customers from other marketing channels?
- Where can more prospects be found for each channel?
- What types of customers are acquired through each channel?
- Which channels produce the most "high-profit" customers?
- What kind of media best produces responses from the targeted profiles?
- How can using different channels maximize exposure to high-profit profiles?

Analyzing marketing channels and making adjustments to them based upon that analysis is the key to successfully changing a company's business model.

Overlay Data

Overlay data (sometimes called *enhancement*) are used when an organization has a database of customers and/or prospects and needs to know more about what the customers/prospects look like. Overlay data are available for both consumer and business databases, and an organization can match their database with a compiler of consumer or business data.

A database compiler gathers compiled consumer or business data. Currently, there are two major compilers of U.S. business data and four major compilers of U.S. consumer data. Outside of the U.S., overlay data availability varies by country, but is typically not available. In addition, there are a variety of smaller compilers that specialize in gathering data for specific industries. In the U.S., consumer compilers have databases listing over 230 million consumers and business compilers list over 15 million businesses.

Business data are collected from many sources including yellow page directories; white pages; blue pages; annual reports; 10-K reports; SEC data; federal, state, and municipal government data; business magazines, top newspapers, new business register data, industry specific data; and more. Virtually every credible public source is used. The business data are verified by telephone, with over 20 million calls a year to validate current information and gather additional marketing information.

Typical overlay data for a business file include primary Standard Industrial Classification (SIC) codes (i.e., business type), sales volume, employee size, actual number of employees, years in business, secondary SIC codes, size of ad(s) in the yellow pages, and corporate parent or subsidiary linkages

Consumer data are compiled from white page telephone directories, property records, real estate deed and assessment information, product registrations, surveys, auto registrations, driver's license information, magazine subscribers, mail-order buyers/responders, and much more. Compilers generally have over 3,000 original public and proprietary sources. In the U.S., these compiled consumer databases are updated regularly through the National Change of Address system maintained by the United States Post Office, along with deceased listings that are based primarily on payments of Social Security death benefits. The national "Do Not Mail" registry is maintained by the Direct Marketing Association, but the Do Not Call registry is maintained by the U.S. Federal Trade Commission (FTC).

Typical overlay data for a consumer file include age, income, home value, whether they are a homeowner or renter, length of residence, whether or not children live in the home, and "neighborhood" variables, such as ethnicity, types of housing, types of employment, and population density.

Overlay data can be obtained directly from the compiler, or through a broker that works with several compilers. The main U.S. compilers, along with a broker, are listed in Exhibit 2.8.

Exhibit 2.8: Primary U.S. Overlay Data Compilers and Brokers

InfoUSA (Consumer and Business Compiler)
Omaha, NE
800-555-5335
www.infousa.com

Experian (Consumer and Business Compiler)
Schaumburg, IL
888-214-4391
www.experian.com

D&B (Business Compiler)
Short Hills, NJ
800-234-3867
www.dnb.com/us/

Equifax (Consumer compiler)
Atlanta, GA
888-685-1111
www.equifax.com

King Marketing Group (Broker for major compilers)
Olathe, KS
913-963-7899
kingmarketing@comcast.net

RUF Strategic Solutions
Olathe, KS
913-782-8544
www.ruf.com

Survey Data

Surveys can add knowledge about already known data. For example, a company manufacturing truck engines knew by fleet which of their customers haul refrigerated food, which have beer trucks, which have general freight, and so on. What they did not know was what this information meant in terms of how heavily the trucks were used.

To help determine truck usage the company surveyed a variety of freight haulers, asking how far their trucks were driven each year and how often the trucks were traded. They learned that over-the-road trucks hauling refrigerated food went the most miles each year, and were traded the most often. Beer trucks went relatively few miles each year and were traded least often.

Applying the knowledge from the survey to the tens of thousands of fleets in their database, this truck engine manufacturer was able to learn more about their clients and prospects without the expense of surveying each one.

On the other hand, a manufacturer of woodworking equipment surveyed all of their customers and asked them questions about their ages and incomes. They found that gathering comparable data through overlay data rather than through surveys was less expensive and produced more accurate data. Instead of eliminating the surveys, the manufacturer revised them and asked questions for which they otherwise would not have the answers. The revised surveys inquired about what other kinds of woodworking equipment the customer had, what kind of woodworking they most enjoyed, and so on. As a result, the manufacturer had a much better picture of its customers than before.

Surveys are not 100 percent accurate and the results can be biased; however, when conducted properly, they can provide a company with useful information.

All methods of describing customers, whether it is through demographic profiling or surveys, are most effective when it is clear which customers are best, which are marginal, and which are only prospects.

Understanding customers and segments of customers based on demographics and lifestyles can be a key in managing the business model. The ability to precisely describe your customer base is necessary before you can begin building a contract strategy.

Learning from Our Customers

When working with transaction-based customer data, you are likely to experience some or all of the following common truisms. Each one represents a possible threat to the current perception of the business model, and taken together, often lead to major changes on how the organization manages customer and prospect relationships.

Compare these "typical" findings to what you think fits your own organization's business model.

- It costs eight to ten times as much to make the first sale to a prospect as it does to make another sale to a customer.

If this weren't true, there would be no reason to track customer relationships. In fact, we often find the cost to make the first sale is higher than ten times the cost to re-sell an existing customer. Spending 20 times as much to sell to a prospect as to re-sell a customer is not uncommon.

The chart in Exhibit 2.9 shows typical costs for a direct marketing firm selling to both businesses and consumers. It is clear that it is much cheaper to sell to customers than it is to sell to prospects.

This has a major impact on organizations that contact prospects and customers the same way or that don't measure the financial results of marketing investments separately between customers and prospects. As a result, the "balance" between prospecting versus re-selling efforts is often sub-optimal in a typical organization.

- A re-contact or re-mailing can get 50 percent of the response of the initial contact.

Exhibit 2.9: Typical Cost to Make a Sale

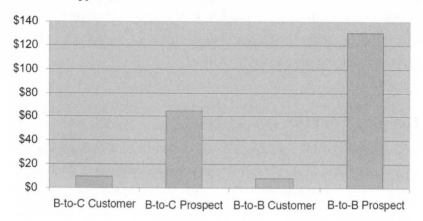

If this weren't true, contacting customers more often wouldn't get more sales, but it does! Customer segments that are responding at twice break-even or above should be contacted more often, even if the communication is basically unchanged. A re-contact to top-performing segments is often the best way to utilize over-run or excess marketing materials.

A customer response rate of 12 percent to a single effort (for example, a letter or catalog) would drop to about 6 percent for a repeat contact in a short time period, and drop to about 3 percent for a third contact. (See Exhibit 2.10.) Note, this "Ah-ha" covers one or two re-contacts. Re-contacting can be overdone!

Fortunately, customers that are more likely to buy are more appropriate to contact more often. As a result, balancing the most appropriate marketing frequency with the most profitable contact frequency often results in little conflict, if any.

- "Advocates" respond much better than "Buyers" and repeat "Buyers" respond much better than one-time "Tryers."

For most organizations, about 80 percent of their revenue comes from 20 percent of their customers. Quite often, it is closer to 90/10. These

Exhibit 2.10: Response Rates for Multiple Contacts

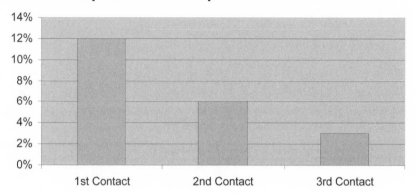

top customers are advocates, and drive the profitability of the organization. They should be contacted most often and most carefully.

Typically, another 25 to 35 percent or so of customers make up about 10 to 15 percent of sales. These are the "buyers." Those that look like advocates may have the potential to be moved up to that group. Ideally, the organization can sell to buyers at break-even or above, when all costs are considered.

For many organizations, 50 to 60 percent of customers provide only 5 to 10 percent of sales. Rarely does this group make a profit for the organization. However, these tryers are an entry point for the organization to find buyers and advocates.

Sales per contact will be much higher for advocates than for buyers or tryers. This has to be true in order for 80 percent of sales to come from 20 percent of the customers.

The example in Exhibit 2.11 shows how advocates are many times more valuable than other customers, based on typical sales per contact for a business-to-consumer direct retailer.

- Alan's Rule of Half-Life: "A segment of customers will drop in response by half each year they do not buy."

Typically, buyers who just made a purchase are twice as likely to respond to a new offer as buyers who have not bought since one year ago.

Exhibit 2.11: Sales per Contact for Advocates, Buyers, and Tryers

One-year-ago buyers are twice as likely to respond as two-year-ago buyers, and so on. Understanding this explains why an organization will contact new customers more often.

As if by magic, this rule holds up again and again in all types of industries, whether fundraising, ticket sales, retail, business-to-business, or even banking services. Clearly, more recent customers respond at a higher rate than customers who haven't made any recent purchases. (See Exhibit 2.12.)

- The biggest single segment in any database is usually one-time buyers of the popular item(s).

Exhibit 2.12: Response Rate Based on Recency

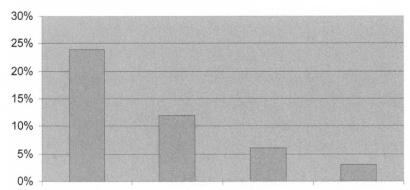

Most organizations know that 50 to 60 percent of their customers are one-time buyers (tryers). Often, what these organizations don't realize is that about half of their one-time buyers have bought only one of their leading items. This tends to be a huge group—one-fourth to one-third of the database. They are easily identified, and they are much harder to re-sell to than one-time buyers who initially purchased more than one item. Having a strategy to deal with them is crucial to gaining more repeat buyers.

Exhibit 2.13 shows counts of one-time buyers from a consumer cata-loger that sells a very popular lead item costing $39.95. It is easy to see from the chart approximately half of their one-time buyers spent exactly $39.95, making them very easy to spot.

- Buyers that spend a small amount on their initial purchase are likely to continue to spend less than average on future purchases.

This is particularly true for organizations that sell business-to-consumer. The amount (per order) that customers have spent in the past is usually an excellent indicator of how much they will spend (per order) in the future. Past average order size is often a better predictor than overall monetary.

This is especially crucial to track when prospects are attracted by a

Exhibit 2.13: Counts of One-Time Buyers by Amount of Sale

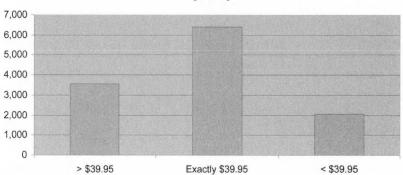

low price—they may not be profitable customers in the future. Many organizations forget this rule and try to attract new customers with low-priced offerings that don't represent what they typically sell to their better repeat customers.

Exhibit 2.14: Average Second Order Amounts by First Order

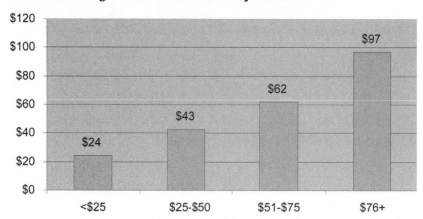

The chart in Exhibit 2.14 is based on a direct retailer with an average order of $65. Clearly, the new customers that started out with a small first order usually did not increase the amount of their next order dramatically. This pattern held for third and subsequent orders as well.

- One-time buyers (tryers) that made a small purchase are often unprofitable to re-contact in 18 months or less.

Many organizations contact all buyers for three years or more and don't segment out one-time buyers with lower first orders. These organizations are often shocked to find they've been marketing to low-potential customer segments unprofitably for years.

Even if one-time buyers as a whole are contacted for several years at a profit, that does not mean small-order one-time buyers within that group are profitable.

Exhibit 2.15 shows how response rates drop quickly for one-time buyers with small first orders, when they are broken out by how long

Exhibit 2.15: Small First Order Response Rates of One-Time Buyers

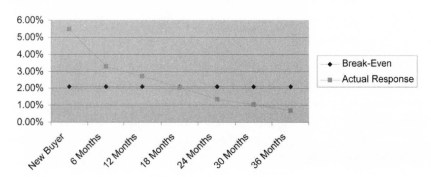

ago they made a purchase. Response drops quickly, and due to typically low average orders, the response rate required to break-even is fairly high. For some, the curve is even faster. It is not uncommon for organizations to gather many customers with a very low cost item, to find they cannot follow them up for over six months, if they can follow them up at all!

- One-time buyers (tryers) are more likely to buy again soon after their first purchase, not long after.

Some organizations are reluctant to follow up quickly with new buyers, perhaps thinking they won't need anything for a while. Others will leave gaps in their re-contact strategy, where a new customer may not receive a follow-up contact for several months. It is rare when an immediate re-contact strategy does not succeed. Better to communicate now, while the first sale is fresh, than to wait until the relationship with the customer is stale.

The chart in Exhibit 2.16 shows how quickly response drops from the initial date of purchase, with response rates dropping from 12 percent to 9.8 percent after just three days, and dropping all the way to 7.9 percent in just four months. Without a follow-up strategy in place, marketers can miss the opportunity for additional sales. For example, many retailers that attract new customers at the November-December holiday

Exhibit 2.16: First-Time Buyer Response Rates by Time Since Initial Order

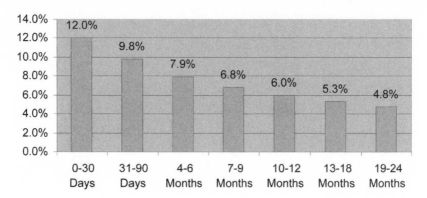

season actually wait until August or September before they start to re-contact them because they don't have a contact plan in place that spans the entire year. A look at the dropping response rate potential highlights the opportunities lost for those who wait.

- Sales-per-contact is a more important indicator than response rate.

This is true for two reasons. First, buyers who spend more are more likely to buy again. Secondly, buyers who spend more are likely to continue to spend more with each future order. Generally speaking, it is more profitable, now and in the future, to get one $100-buyer than to get two $50-buyers.

The table shows responses from three lists, each with very different results. List A had the highest response rate, but it had an average order

	Response Rate	Average Order	Sales-per-Contact
List A	5%	$40	$2.00
List B	4%	$60	$2.40
List C	3%	$90	$2.70

of only $40, while list C had a response rate of only 3 percent, but it had the highest average order of $90.

Of the three, list C was actually the best. Sales-per-contact (response rate times average order) was $2.70 for list C, but only $2.00 for list A. In other words, for every person contacted, list C brought in $2.70 (on average) and list A brought in $2.00.

Many organizations focus too much on response rates, when they should focus on how effectively they are making contacts. When sales are more important than just responses, sales-per-contact is a better measure.

- There is no relationship between customer acquisition cost in different media/channels and the future value of customers acquired through different media/channels.

Marketers in many organizations measure only acquisition cost, source-by-source, and ignore lifetime value. But quite often there is a big gap in follow-up purchase behavior between customers acquired through retail, catalog, the Web, or other media. Simply measuring acquisition cost is not enough, as profits come from repeat sales.

Be sure that those customers acquired through different media become good customers. Do not assume customers acquired through new media will behave the same as customers acquired through older, tested media. They may be better or they may be worse. Keep in mind that results by media are often counterintuitive.

Results often seem counterintuitive because marketers usually expect people acquired through their "main" channel to be most valuable. For example, a cataloger attracting new customers through both catalogs and direct-TV would expect customers acquired through direct-TV to buy less through the catalog in the future. This may or may not be so. The only thing you can be sure of is that in order to understand the buying habits of customers across different media you must track customers' buying across different media. Take nothing for granted and assume nothing will fit preconceived notions.

- When organizations serve both businesses and consumers, businesses typically have a higher acquisition cost, but also typically have a lifetime value eight to ten times (or more) higher than consumers.

It is more difficult to gain businesses than consumers as clients, but the payoff can be much higher.

Businesses may spend more by making more frequent or larger purchases and are more loyal. Be sure to measure follow-up sales with businesses and not just acquisition cost. Mark customers as business or consumer, so it is easy to differentiate them in the database.

The graph in Exhibit 2.17 shows results from a company with a substantial difference in acquisition costs for businesses and consumers, but an even greater difference in lifetime value. An investment in acquiring new business customers will pay greater dividends over time than an investment in acquiring consumers. Interestingly, many marketers measure only acquisition cost, and not lifetime value. Such a marketer would likely target only consumers and leave the more profitable businesses to their competition.

- Businesses may buy more often than consumers, but may not buy more at once.

Exhibit 2.17: Acquisition Cost and Lifetime Value of Consumer and Business Customers

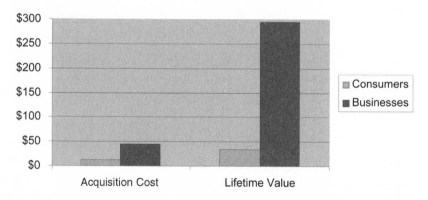

For many who sell business-to-business, a huge share of their orders are from customers who make small, frequent purchases. Sometimes called the "$50 Every Two Weeks" rule, it appears many people can make small orders ($50 or less) every two weeks or so without special authorization from senior staff. Out of convenience, these customers make many small orders to avoid the paperwork of one big order.

Business-to-business marketers need to look at the number and size of their orders, not just the average order. If an organization cannot process small orders profitably, this could be a problem.

Exhibit 2.18: Number of Orders by Order Amount

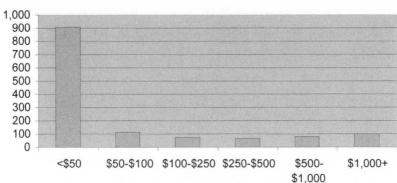

The graph in Exhibit 2.18 is taken from a business-to-business company with an average order of $500 and shows the count of orders by amount. Clearly, that is not their "typical" order. Most orders are less than $50, and they likely lose money on each of them.

- Business customers that have more than one contact and buy more than one category of item or service are mostly likely to be loyal.

This is true regardless of the amount of money a customer has spent in the past. For some business-to-business sellers, attrition rates for buyers with multiple contacts, buying in multiple categories is near zero for the company as a whole.

Exhibit 2.19: Average Annual Spending by Number of Buying Contacts

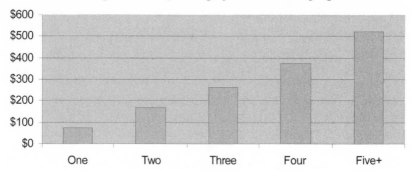

Business customers with multiple contacts are not only more likely to become more loyal as more contacts begin to buy, they become more valuable at an accelerating rate. Based on an office supply company, Exhibit 2.19 shows that two people buy more than twice as one, three people buy more than three times as much as one, and so on. Apparently, buy-in from multiple contacts serves several purposes for sellers.

- Free first purchases may not produce your best customers in the long-term.

While a free first purchase offer may seem like a good way to attract new customers or to develop customer loyalty, over the long-term this

Exhibit 2.20: Comparison of Free vs. Paid First Purchases

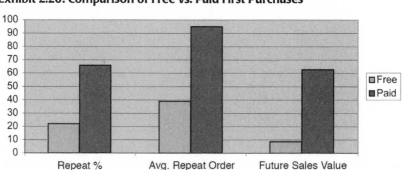

usually does not prove true. Exhibit 2.20 shows data from a photo studio in which repeat purchases were made by only 22 percent of customers whose initial purchase was "free," meaning they got the service but paid nothing at all. Compared to a 66 percent repeat purchase rate of those who paid for their initial purchase, this free offer appears to dramatically reduce loyalty. Similarly, in terms of dollars, the repeat average purchases of those whose initial first purchase was free amounted to less than half ($39.00 versus $95.00) that of those who paid for their initial purchase. Long-term, the future sales value of the "free first purchase" group is significantly less ($9.00 versus $63.00) than that of the "paid first purchase" group.

	Repeat Purchase Percent	Average Repeat in Dollars	Future Sales Value
Free First Purchase	22%	$39.00	$9.00
Paid First Purchase	66%	$95.00	$63.00

Describing What Customers Do

To understand what customers do, it is necessary to begin with a clear understanding of cause and effect. In the simplest terms, organizations create a stimulus (an offer, an advertisement) in order to gain a response (a sale, a request for further information). Attempting to assign cause and effect to related variables beyond the organization's control may be interesting for academics, but it is of no practical use for marketers.

Database marketing, or any marketing, is at its core based on stimulus and response. In general marketing, the response can be measured in aggregate, such as at a store or regional level. In database marketing, stimulus and response can be measured at the individual level for each customer and prospect.

The business model should coincide with the effectiveness of the stimuli the organization sends to customers and prospects. For example, if the organization is targeting offers to companies with 50 or more employees, and then finds most of its customers have 15 or fewer employees, the stimuli should be re-directed to a more appropriate audience.

Correlated variables can be helpful, if they can better target an audience. For example, married couples age 30 to 35 with two or more kids may be more likely than most people to buy a minivan. While this is a useful piece of information, it still falls to the organization to develop suitable stimuli to attract this audience and measure their response.

Tracking Behavior

For many organizations, the greatest challenge in using data to drive the business model is tracking the relationship of stimuli and responses.

For classic direct marketers, such as catalogers, it is relatively simple. Each stimulus (catalog) is marked with a specific key code that represents the segment the recipient was in at the time the stimuli was created. When the operator asks you for that code (usually with a question like "What is the number in the blue box on the back of the catalog?") she is connecting the correct stimulus to your response.

Key code information is not available for most other point-of-sale systems. Many retailers and salespeople will simply ask, "How did you hear about us?" While they don't always get accurate answers, it sometimes helps. However, some retailers don't wish to pry for customer information, especially when many customers don't like it.

Many marketers keep the lists of names they sent offers to and will later match those lists against actual buyers. This can be done by a unique customer ID or by matching name and address through a merge/purge style process. This back-end matching process is called a *back test*. A back test is the most common way to gather response data when it is possible to track each sale to a specific customer, but impossible to gather key codes.

Some retailers don't send advertising to test segments of customers or test segments of stores and markets, and then measure results of those who did receive advertising versus those who did not. Some go so far as to hold advertising back for some customers at each promotion (changing test segments from promotion to promotion) and having another segment that doesn't get any promotions for a year to test the combined value of all the promotions.

Before building a database to track customer behavior, or more specifically, the relationship of the organization's stimuli to the customers' responses, there must be a clear understanding of how it can be tracked. Before the computers are purchased, before the software is installed, you must have a clear understanding of how you will track, and make sure the systems put in place do track. Otherwise, the relationship of stimuli and response will remain unknown and the database will be worthless.

Measuring Lift

Measuring the effectiveness of an offer (stimulus) sometimes demands measuring something called *lift*. Lift is the amount of increased response a stimulus makes above what would have happened anyway, without that particular stimulus.

For example, let's go back to the married couples, ages 30 to 35, with two kids. Let's say for every 10,000 such households in the U.S., 125 buy a Dodge minivan each year, without any specific marketing effort.

Now let's say we isolate 20,000 of these households, and send 10,000 of them an offer for a free DVD player with the purchase of a Dodge minivan. We don't send anything to the other 10,000 households.

We track the offer, and one year later 200 people that received the DVD offer bought a Dodge minivan and 125 of the people who did not receive anything bought a Dodge minivan.

So, did the offer sent to the first 10,000 households sell 200 minivans or did it sell 75? Marketers will be disappointed to find out they should get credit for only 75. The offer generated a lift of 75 sales over no offer.

Lift is an especially important thing to measure when comparing marginal offers. For example, if an offer that needs a 1 percent response rate to break-even actually gets a 1 percent response rate, it is worth asking "would people have bought anyway?" Did the offer add enough sales over what would have come in without it to make business sense?

If the target audience would have purchased at a 0.5 percent rate with no offer, the answer is no. The offer created a "lift" of only 0.5 percent, not 1.0 percent. If the target audience would not have responded without an offer, the answer is yes. The offer adds just enough sales to break-even.

Break-Even(s)

Break-even is more than just a useful calculation for determining if a campaign has exceeded a basic financial goal. It is a useful planning tool, necessary for understanding how campaigns should be devised.

The purpose of any marketing campaign is (or should be) to meet or exceed a basic financial goal. Few organizations will be satisfied with campaigns that cost more money in the long-term than they generate in revenue. Only in cases where lifetime value (future profits from repeat sales) outweighs any short-term loss will below break-even efforts make sense.

An early goal for any team doing business modeling should be to determine the basic break-even level that the marketing efforts must achieve to be profitable and the level below which they lose money. Simply doing the calculation and comparing necessary results to actual results often makes for a real shock. Many organizations run many campaigns at a loss and if they have not tracked results or held marketing accountable to some minimum standard, it is not uncommon for them to be unaware of the problem.

As a general rule, if marketing is creating campaigns and does not know what the break-even level is, they are not trying to achieve a specific financial goal. In other words, if people haven't stopped to determine what the break-even level is, and whether or not campaigns are exceeding it, it is a good bet they are not making any attempt at profitable, accountable marketing. They may have a stack of awards for creative and original advertising, but unless your organization is an advertising agency, that rarely helps to improve the bottom line.

Break-even is relatively easy to calculate, and for the sake of simplicity we will assume we are looking only at variable cost. In other words, we won't worry about things like overhead, managers' salaries, and so on.

In order to estimate break-even, it is necessary to know:

- Average order amount (a typical or mean sale amount)
- Returns and/or cancellations percentage
- Bad debt percentage
- Cost-of-goods sold percentage
- Fulfillment cost (cost to take an order)
- Cost per reach

Case Study: Variable Break-Even

A company selling stuffed bears is trying to get more customers to return to their stores and make repeat purchases. Their goal is to make a positive contribution to overhead and profit by contacting customers, but at a very minimum they must break-even on any promotion. In other words, they need to at least cover the variable costs of marketing and selling.

They have been sending customers colorful mailings with pictures of the various bears and other stuffed toys at the holiday, on the customer's birthday, and occasionally off-season to drive traffic to their stores. Each mailing costs about 75 cents to produce and mail.

The company has an average order of approximately $35.00 and each bear costs about $17.50 to produce. So, cost-of-goods sold is about 50 percent. In addition, their returns and cancellations run about 2 percent of sales and their bad debt about 0.5 percent (one-half of a percent) of sales. It costs the company around $4.00 per sale to wrap, package, and sell each bear.

During the holidays, they average about a 9 percent response rate from previous customers. For birthdays, they do even better, about an 11.5 percent response rate. The occasional off-season promotions produce about a 4.5 percent response rate.

Overall, the company's marketing department is proud of their results since they have been told anything over 2 percent is good. However, the

Exhibit 3.1a: Variable Break-Even

Category	Amount
Average Order	**$54.95**
Returns or Cancellations	**6.00%**
Bad Debt	**3.00%**
Net Merchandise Sales	$50.00
Cost of Goods Sold %	**50.00%**
Fulfillment Cost per Order	**$5.00**
Advertising Cost per Reach	**$1.00**
Break-Even Response %	5.00%
Break-Even $ per Name	$2.50

CFO wants to know if they are exceeding their goal of break-even during the holidays, with birthday promotions, and off-season.

A break-even spreadsheet is included on the accompanying CD-ROM (select the Excel Workbook tab labeled "Break Even") and the figures are also provided in Exhibit 3.1a. Apply the figures in the case to determine:

- Which promotions, (holiday, birthday, and off-season), if any, at least break-even?
- What is the minimum break-even point the company must achieve?
- Would you change or eliminate any of the promotions based on your results?

If you performed the calculations in Exhibit 3.1a, you should be able to respond to the three questions as follows:

- Which promotions, if any (holiday, birthday, and off-season) at least break-even?

  Holiday gets a 9 percent response, and birthday gets a 1.5 percent response, so those two perform above break-even.

- What is the minimum break-even point the company must achieve?

  5.74 percent or $1.96 in sales per name mailed

- Would you change or eliminate any of the promotions based on your results?

  Off-season performs at 4.5 percent, which is below break-even, so it should be changed or eliminated.

If you filled in the spreadsheet correctly, it should look like this:

Exhibit 3.1b: Variable Break-Even

Category	Amount
Average Order	**$35.00**
Returns or Cancellations	**2.00%**
Bad Debt	**0.50%**
Net Merchandise Sales	$34.13
Cost of Goods Sold %	**50.00%**
Fulfillment Cost per Order	**$4.00**
Advertising Cost per Reach	**$0.75**
Break-Even Response %	5.74%
Break-Even $ per Name	$1.96

In this example, a 5 percent response rate is required to break-even. For a marketer typically getting a 10 percent response rate, this would be good news. For someone typically getting a 1 percent response rate, this is bad news.

Note the break-even dollar per name is $2.50. That is the average order multiplied by the response percentage. Generally, dollar per name is a better overall measure than response rate alone, since it incorporates both response rate and average order.

For those who want to appear smart at cocktail parties, there is the "back of the napkin" way to calculate break-even. To use it, determine (or estimate) two things:

1. How much profit (margin) is made with each order?
2. How much is cost per reach?

In the example in Exhibit 3.1a, the company makes about $20 profit per order (after fulfillment costs). Cost per reach is $1.00.

OK, take out your napkin. A $1.00 (cost-per-reach) divided by $20 (profit per order) is 5 percent. That's it—cost per reach divided by profit per order: a quick, easy data check for any proposed campaign.

Fulfillment cost, or the fixed cost of taking each order, is usually ignored, but it should not be. It includes the cost of things like in-bound phone calls, boxes, bags, labels, receipts, and so on. Most organizations underestimate fulfillment cost. As a guide, consider that the average direct-mail catalog loses an average of about seven dollars on fulfillment, over and above what they collect for shipping and handling. The cost of fulfillment is why, for many businesses, some orders are literally too small to be profitable.

Consider the business-to-business seller with an average order of $500. A few large orders raised the average, but 80 percent of orders were $50 or less. Their low margins were not enough to overcome fulfillment cost on orders under $50. They had to re-focus their organization toward making larger sales and avoiding smaller ones.

A large specialty retailer was using direct mail to drive traffic to stores. They analyzed their results and found they were getting a near 1 percent response. They did this for over a year before someone did a simple break-even analysis and realized that with their typical average sale and typical profit margin they need over 2 percent. As a result, they stopped using direct mail for prospects, which typically responded below 1 percent, and shifted more mailings to customers, which typically responded at 5 percent to 10 percent. The following year, same store sales rose nearly 50 percent.

The break-even functions largely as a reality check. Many bad ideas would never have gotten off the drawing boards if the break-evens were calculated sooner.

Profitability by Campaign

Profitability by campaign is the next logical extension of break-even. It's great to know break-even is 5 percent if the organization has been gathering a 10 percent response, but if the goal is to make a profit, what then?

If you have what you need to create a break-even, then there are only a few more things to know to develop profitability by campaign. They are:

- Total sales (either expected if planning or actual if measuring)
- Cost to design advertising (would be zero if you re-use existing materials)
- Cost of printing or placement (the cost to mail, get space in a magazine, buy TV spots, etc.)

Corporate marketing managers are typically charged with making a certain profit or contribution to overhead and profit. Sometimes this is a percentage and sometimes this is a specific amount.

Before a campaign, a spreadsheet can be used to determine if the campaign seems likely to meet its goals. Perhaps more advertising is necessary to cover fixed costs or if average order could be increased, then goals could be reached.

Case Study: Profitability by Campaign

A business-to-business seller of woodworking equipment is trying to improve its profitability by selling more consumable items like sandpaper, shapers, and finishing tools to customers.

They believe their promotions have been performing well above break-even, but they don't really know by how much. The CFO has asked marketing to set a goal of a contribution to overhead and profit of 10 percent of sales for each campaign.

Marketing has put together some figures based on their last campaign to determine if they are reaching the goal. First, they know gross sales totaled $150,000. About 1 percent of the items is typically returns or cancels, 1 percent is usually lost due to bad debt on accounts, and cost-of-goods sold runs about 57 percent. Orders averaged $125 and fulfillment cost was $10 per order. They spent $5,000 to create advertising for the promotion and $35,000 actually running the ads.

A sample spreadsheet is included on the CD-ROM (select the Excel Workbook tab labeled "Profitability by Campaign") and the figures are also provided in Exhibit 3.2a. Based on the numbers provided, determine:

- Did they make the goal the CFO set?
- How much did they make in dollars and as a percent of sales?

Exhibit 3.2a: Profitability by Campaign

Category	Amount	% of Net Sales
Gross Sales	$ 105,000	104.17%
Returns or Cancellations	$ 2,100	2.00%
Bad Debt	$ 2,100	2.00%
Net Sales	$ 100,800	100.00%
Cost of Goods	$ 50,400	50.00%
Average Order	$ 75.00	
Fulfillment Cost per Order	$ 7.00	
Total Fulfillment	$ 9,800	9.72%
Design of Advertising (fixed)	$ 5,000	4.96%
Advertising Printing or Placement (variable)	$ 25,000	24.80%
Contribution to Overhead & Profit	$ 10,600	10.52%

- If they had spent $70,000 on advertising placement and sales were $295,000, would they have made or exceeded the goal? (all other numbers being equal)
- Which would you recommend based on the above situations: Spending $70,000 on advertising and getting sales of $295,000 or spending $35,000 on advertising and getting sales of $150,000?

If you performed the calculations in Exhibit 3.2a, you should be able to respond to the four questions as follows:

- Did they make the goal the CFO set?

    The goal was 10 percent contribution to profit and overhead. The campaign achieved 7.63 percent, so the answer is no.

- How much did they make in dollars and as a percent of sales?

    They made $11,210 and 7.63 percent of sales.

- If they had spent $70,000 on advertising placement and sales were $295,000, would they have made or exceeded the goal? (all other numbers being equal)

  They would have done better, with a contribution to profit and overhead of 8.89 percent and profit dollars of $25,713, but they still would not have exceeded 10 percent contribution to profit and overhead.

- Which would you recommend based on the above situations: Spending $70,000 on advertising and getting sales of $295,000 or spending $35,000 on advertising and getting sales of $150,000?

  If the money were available for more advertising placement, spending $70,000 and getting $295,000 in sales produces a greater total profit and a higher profit as a percentage of sales.

If you filled out the spreadsheet correctly for the first scenario ($35,000 in placement, $150,000 in sales) it should look like Exhibit 3.2b.

Exhibit 3.2b: Profitability by Campaign

Category	Amount	% of Net Sales
Gross Sales	$ 150,000	102.04%
Returns or Cancellations	$ 1,500	1.00%
Bad Debt	$ 1,500	1.00%
Net Sales	$ 147,000	100.00%
Cost of Goods	$ 83,790	57.00%
Average Order	$ 125.00	
Fulfillment Cost per Order	$ 10.00	
Total Fulfillment	$ 12,000	8.16%
Design of Advertising (fixed)	$ 5,000	3.40%
Advertising Printing or Placement (variable)	$ 35,000	23.81%
Contribution to Overhead & Profit	$ 11,210	7.63%

If you filled out the spreadsheet correctly for the second scenario ($70,000 in placement, $295,000 in sales) it should look like Exhibit 3.2c:

Exhibit 3.2c: Profitability by Campaign

Category	Amount	% of Net Sales
Gross Sales	$ 295,000	102.04%
Returns or Cancellations	$ 2,950	1.00%
Bad Debt	$ 2,950	1.00%
Net Sales	$ 289,100	100.00%
Cost of Goods	$ 164,787	57.00%
Average Order	$ 125.00	
Fulfillment Cost per Order	$ 10.00	
Total Fulfillment	$ 23,600	8.16%
Design of Advertising (fixed)	$ 5,000	1.73%
Advertising Printing or Placement (variable)	$ 70,000	24.21%
Contribution to Overhead & Profit	$ 25,713	8.89%

The spreadsheet can be used for either estimating a dollar profit, or a percentage of sales, or both. After campaigns are over, actual results can be compared to estimates.

Estimating profit by campaign allows marketers to mix up high-profit customers and low- (or no-) profit prospects. Combining results by campaign also allows marketers to determine progress toward an annual goal. As a general rule, annual profits generated by marketing should more than cover any overhead associated with marketing.

For example, the specialty retailer in the break-even example also wanted to set a target for contribution to overhead and profit of 20 percent. They realized they were losing a great deal of money sending mail to prospects and were getting nearly a 40 percent return from customer mailings so, they readjusted their mail plans. By increasing customer mailings, they increased the overall profit and by reducing prospect mailings, they reduced overall loss. Balancing the two to reach a goal of 20 percent allowed them to maximize the prospecting they could afford to do to bring in new customers, while ensuring they earned enough profit to run the business.

For those of you outside of marketing, consider it a serious warning if your marketing department cannot or does not calculate some version of either breakeven or profitability by campaign. If they are not doing so, they are not managing to financially accountable goals.

Predictive Modeling

As discussed in Chapter Two, predictive modeling is very different than descriptive modeling. The goals of predictive modeling are to determine how likely customers and prospects are to respond (response rate) or the degree to which they will likely respond (how much they will spend). The goal of descriptive modeling is simply to better understand the marketplace.

In other words, predictive modeling is more useful for determining with whom you should speak; descriptive modeling is more useful for determining what you should say. Predictive modeling is best used for selection/de-selection of customers and potential customers in future communication efforts. Descriptive modeling is the better choice for showing differences and similarities among customers and potential customers that help you create different messages or offers for different customers and prospects. You should be aware that because predictive modeling and descriptive modeling are such different processes, they tend to arrive at completely different results. Do not expect similar segments and do not expect the two to easily fit together.

When we talk about using statistical models to improve return on investment (ROI), we are generally talking about using predictive models. Predictive models are specifically focused on who should or should not be contacted and, as a result, measuring the results of using the model is simple. A sample of non-target customers or prospects can be included in a campaign for comparison to targets and the difference in response can be measured.

Predictive modeling will tend to rely most heavily on transactional data when it is available because past purchase behavior tends to drown out other variables the model may use. However, demographic and behavioral characteristics of a company's best customers can be used in a predictive model for identifying qualified prospects. Prospects can be from "house" lists of non-buyers or from a rented or purchased list of some sort. Remember, past behavior is the best predictor of future behavior.

The results from the predictive modeling process are based entirely upon the data. Opinion and other biases are not a part of this kind of analysis. The intention is to have results that can be safely used to predict future prospect behavior. If the results are politically incorrect within the organization at least they are based on fact, reproducible, and consistent.

Predictive modeling analysis relies primarily upon accurate response, sales, and margin data for its effectiveness. Good data and a thorough understanding of customer behavior are essential for success. That is why it is often the last (and most sophisticated) of the marketing analysis techniques discussed.

For a business modeling team, it is usually a good idea to get to predictive modeling later rather than earlier in the analytical process because those within the organization who dislike the results will need to find something to attack and the most likely target are the data used to create the predictive model. In addition, predictive models have the political disadvantage of seeming mysterious, and because they tend to be highly complex methods, are often difficult to explain. If you plan on driving change with predictive modeling, plan on using accurate data that has been thoroughly checked, as more sophisticated techniques tend to uncover more deeply hidden problems. Data check the predictive model's results thoroughly before using them or presenting them to potentially hostile management.

Predictive modeling can use a variety of statistical techniques. These include regression analysis, CHAID (Chi-Square Automatic Interaction Detector) and C&RT (Classification and Regression Tree) among others. Each technique is better for certain types of predictions. Be sure to have an expert available who knows how to select the right tool for the job. Each tool, such as CHAID or cluster analysis, can be the best tool in some circumstance, but no tool is best in all circumstances. It is better to hire an analyst capable of using a variety of tools and well able to discern which tool is best for your circumstance, than to hire a firm touting a specific tool.

A *regression analysis* is a technique that applies a score reflecting the predicted likelihood or degree of statistical conformance to each record. *Linear regression* is commonly used to predict the degree of an occurrence, such as predicted order amount. *Log linear regression* is commonly used to predict the likelihood of an occurrence, such as predicted response rate. A non-business example of linear regression is that it could be used to predict how much it is likely to rain, while log linear regression could be used to predict how likely it is to rain.

Both *CHAID* and *C&RT* are predictive models that create a "tree diagram" where customers and prospects are divided into mutually exclusive segments. They tend to be viewed as having similarities to descriptive models since segments are easily definable and easily understood. However, do not expect similar results.

Another impact of predictive modeling, which is a by-product of shrinking the number of potential customers through better targeting, is allowing for multiple contacts. An organization might have contacted 250,000 people once a year. After determining through modeling the target audience might be only 100,000 people, the organization can instead reach 100,000 once, 50,000 twice, 25,000 people three times, and so on. Generally speaking, the more likely a segment is to respond, the more times it can be contacted. By using repeat contacts to best segments, they can actually increase sales while employing fewer total contacts.

The complexity of each of these analytical tools ranges from simple (profiling) through complex (predictive modeling), so for effective modeling, it is important to let the task dictate the tool. The cost of performing each type of analysis varies with the complexity and amount of outside data needed, too.

Always begin with a simple cross-tab profiling analysis. Even this simple analysis provides substantial benefits over doing no analysis at all. After you've done your cross-tab analysis, then conduct the more sophisticated analyses when or if they are justified by the cost and complexity of your marketing efforts. The larger your marketing investment, the more you should invest in making the best possible decisions about your offer, your media, and your targets.

Each analytical tool has its place as part of a marketing program. If a simple analysis is not answering questions about how to improve marketing communications, consider using a more sophisticated tool.

Advocates, Buyers, and Tryers

Advocates, buyers, and tryers analysis is an expansion on the traditional Recency-Frequency-Monetary (RFM) analysis.

For many, the use of RFM, the direct marketer's tried-and-true favorite analysis and segmentation technique, needs to be re-thought. Recent research has revealed that looking at customer behavior in just these three dimensions may miss some truly strategic insights.

A new multi-dimensional scoring technique called *ABT Analysis* can uncover things that RFM misses. *ABT* (Advocate, Buyer, Tryer) analysis expands upon the RFM technique, but does not replace it. Like a more powerful telescope, ABT scans the vast amounts of data stored by companies today to provide even deeper customer insights.

For example, business-to-business enterprises often use RFM to identify who buys the most, who buys often, and who bought recently. What RFM tends to miss is:

- Who buys from multiple product categories?
- Which client has one versus several contacts that have purchased?
- Which customers have untapped subsidiaries that have never bought?

RFM vs. RFA Analyses

A recent business-to-business dot.com client asked a common question: where should we deploy our sales force in order to get a higher return on investment? It is interesting to compare the results of a traditional RFM analysis to those of a newer RFA (average order) analysis. The RFA analysis quickly *disproved* two things.

First, higher *Monetary* scores were not always better. The RFA analysis showed that in many cases a high monetary score reflected large numbers of small-dollar sales. The RFM analysis overlooked this fact. Typically, about 20 percent of customers that look like advocates based on RFM are not based on RFA. They place too many small orders and the company actually loses money selling to them.

Second, higher *Frequency* scores were not always better. Again, RFA analysis showed that the frequent small-dollar purchases actually cost the company more to fulfill than the less frequent, high-dollar sales. The RFM analysis missed this point.

So, the individual that the RFM analysis might have defined as a good customer actually had a good chance of being an unprofitable customer. Using a traditional RFM analysis alone, the sales force would have been directed to pursue clients that would be better served by telemarketing and direct mail efforts.

There are two other reasons RFA is superior to RFM.

1. Monetary is Average Sale multiplied by Frequency. RFA separates average order from frequency and avoids confounding these two variables.
2. RFA allows for better targeting of offers to customers with multiple purchases. It avoids sending buyers who have made many $50 purchases offers designed to appeal to buyers typically spending $500. Better offer targeting alone can often increase sales by 10 percent to 20 percent.

Case Study: Recency-Frequency-Average Order (RFA)

This case involves a catalog company that sells to pet owners, breeders, and dog groomers. They sell a wide variety of products, with catalogs typically having 144 to 172 pages. They have an average order of $65, and approximately a 2 percent break-even point. They prefer not to reach customers below break-even.

The CD-ROM contains a spreadsheet in the Excel Workbook (select the tab labeled "Recency Frequency Average Order"); Exhibit 3.3a also provides the data. It contains a sample RFA Segmentation chart which shows the Recency-Frequency-Average Order segments of buyers that received the company's last catalog, along with their responses.

First, let's review how to read the chart:

- Each Recency segment, shown as rows going across, made their last purchase in the time frame specified on the left, before the catalog was mailed. That is, 0 to 30-day Recency buyers made their most recent purchase 0 to 30 days before the mailing list was pulled for the catalog.
- Buyers are placed into the Frequency columns based on

whether they have made one, two, or three or more purchases.

- Within each set of Frequency columns are three Monetary columns, depending on how much each buyers has spent on average in the past.

For example, there are 1,350 buyers (note upper left cell) who made a purchase 0 to 30 days before the list was pulled for the offer being tracked. They spent less than $50 and had made only one purchase in total when the new list was created. This group responded at an 8.10 percent rate, and sales per contact were $3.24.

There are 16,302 buyers who made their last purchase more than 60 months ago, spent less than $50, and had made only one purchase. (See bottom left cell.) This "older" Recency and lower Average Order group responded at 0.51 percent, or only $0.20 per contact.

One of their unique selling propositions is that the owners of the company are licensed veterinarians. Unlike other pet catalogs, they can fill medical prescriptions, including vaccines. Typically, buyers who vaccinate their animal(s) themselves are different than those who take their animal(s) to the veterinarian. Prescription buyers spend the most per order with the company and are the most loyal.

The catalog serves the owners of all kinds of animals, but most of the sales are for dog products, with the next largest segment being cat products. Dog owners in general spend more than cat owners and are more likely to make a repeat purchase.

Business is somewhat seasonal, with sales peaking in the spring (the spring catalog has the highest sales) and again in the late fall (the fall catalog has the next highest sales).

Presently, the company sends four catalogs per year to every customer who made any purchase in the past five years. There is no special loyalty program, no special first-time buyer program, and no special retention program for buyers who have not purchased recently.

Note in the RFA sample chart how quickly response drops in the first 12 months. One-time buyers responded differently from two-time and three-time plus buyers, even when in the same Recency row. There is a difference in response from lower to higher Monetary buyers. The overall retention rate is much higher with three-time plus buyers, who are less likely to stop buying than one-time buyers. The more the company can move one-time buyers into the two-time category, and the more two-time buyers they can convert to three-time plus buyers, the better future customer responses are likely to be.

In order to break even, the company must have at least $2.00 per contact. Using the RFA Segmentation chart provided, make recommendations for the following:

- Would you market to all new first-time buyers the same way?
- To which customers would you send retention offers before they become unprofitable?
- Would you change frequency of contact for most loyal or most recent buyers?
- Would you change frequency of contact to less loyal or less recent buyers?
- Would you make different offers for lower average order buyers vs. higher average order buyers?
- If you found that as a group dog, cat, and veterinary buyers had very different average orders, would you create a different sheet for each?
- When you would stop marketing to a customer (if ever) short of five years?

Hint: You can copy the RFA chart and mark your answers by coloring on the chart.

If you performed the calculations in Exhibit 3.2a, you should be able to respond to the seven questions with the following spreadsheet:

Exhibit 3.3a: Recency-Frequency-Average Order

RECENCY		Frequency=1 Average Order Range:			Frequency=2 Average Order Range:			Frequency=3+ Average Order Range:		
		0-$49	$50-$99	$100+	0-$49	$50-$99	$100+	0-$49	$50-$99	$100+
0-30 DAYS	Contacts	1,350	450	360	675	338	321	293	899	1,347
	$/Contact	$3.24	$6.68	$14.18	$4.63	$11.06	$18.82	$7.13	$17.01	$28.96
	% Response	8.10%	8.91%	11.34%	11.58%	14.74%	15.06%	17.82%	22.68%	23.17%
31-90 DAYS	Contacts	2,612	871	697	1,306	653	620	568	1,179	1,724
	$/Contact	$2.76	$5.69	$12.08	$3.95	$9.42	$16.03	$6.07	$14.49	$24.67
	% Response	6.90%	7.59%	9.66%	9.87%	12.56%	12.83%	15.18%	19.32%	19.73%
4-6 MONTHS	Contacts	3,811	1,270	1,016	1,906	953	905	828	845	1,057
	$/Contact	$2.44	$5.03	$10.68	$3.49	$8.33	$14.17	$5.37	$12.81	$21.81
	% Response	6.10%	6.71%	8.54%	8.72%	11.10%	11.34%	13.42%	17.08%	17.45%
7-9 MONTHS	Contacts	3,916	1,305	1,044	1,958	979	930	851	869	1,086
	$/Contact	$2.00	$4.13	$8.75	$2.86	$6.83	$11.62	$4.40	$10.50	$17.88
	% Response	5.00%	5.50%	7.00%	7.15%	9.10%	9.30%	11.00%	14.00%	14.30%
10-12 MONTHS	Contacts	4,002	1,334	1,067	2,001	1,001	950	870	888	1,110
	$/Contact	$1.62	$3.34	$7.09	$2.32	$5.53	$9.41	$3.56	$8.51	$14.48
	% Response	4.05%	4.46%	5.67%	5.79%	7.37%	7.53%	8.91%	11.34%	11.58%
13-18 MONTHS	Contacts	7,950	2,650	2,120	3,975	1,988	1,888	1,728	1,764	2,204
	$/Contact	$1.24	$2.56	$5.43	$1.77	$4.23	$7.20	$2.73	$6.51	$11.08
	% Response	3.10%	3.41%	4.34%	4.43%	5.64%	5.76%	6.82%	8.68%	8.87%
19-24 MONTHS	Contacts	8,120	2,707	2,165	4,060	2,030	1,929	1,765	1,801	2,252
	$/Contact	$1.00	$2.06	$4.38	$1.43	$3.41	$5.81	$2.20	$5.25	$8.94
	% Response	2.50%	2.75%	3.50%	3.58%	4.55%	4.65%	5.50%	7.00%	7.15%
25-36 MONTHS	Contacts	7,653	2,551	2,041	3,827	1,913	1,818	1,664	2,198	1,622
	$/Contact	$0.76	$1.57	$3.33	$1.09	$2.59	$4.42	$1.67	$3.99	$6.79
	% Response	1.90%	2.09%	2.66%	2.72%	3.46%	3.53%	4.18%	5.32%	5.43%
37-48 MONTHS	Contacts	15,347	5,116	4,093	7,674	3,837	3,645	3,336	2,404	2,255
	$/Contact	$0.48	$0.99	$2.10	$0.69	$1.64	$2.79	$1.06	$2.52	$4.29
	% Response	1.20%	1.32%	1.68%	1.72%	2.18%	2.23%	2.64%	3.36%	3.43%
49-60 MONTHS	Contacts	14,391	4,797	3,838	7,196	3,598	3,418	3,128	2,192	1,990
	$/Contact	$0.28	$0.58	$1.23	$0.40	$0.96	$1.63	$0.62	$1.47	$2.50
	% Response	0.70%	0.77%	0.98%	1.00%	1.27%	1.30%	1.54%	1.96%	2.00%
60 MONTHS+	Contacts	16,302	5,434	4,347	8,151	4,076	3,872	3,544	2,616	2,520
	$/Contact	$0.20	$0.42	$0.89	$0.29	$0.70	$1.19	$0.45	$1.07	$1.82
	% Response	0.51%	0.56%	0.71%	0.73%	0.93%	0.95%	1.12%	1.43%	1.46%

Exhibit 3.3b: Recency-Frequency-Average Order

RECENCY		Frequency=1 Average Order Range:			Frequency=2 Average Order Range:			Frequency=3+ Average Order Range:		
		0-$49	$50-$99	$100+	0-$49	$50-$99	$100+	0-$49	$50-$99	$100+
0-30 DAYS	Customers	1,350	450	360	675	338	321	293	899	1,347
	$/Name	$3.24	$6.68	$14.18	$4.63	$11.06	$18.82	$7.13	$17.01	$28.96
	% Response	8.10%	8.91%	11.34%	11.58%	14.74%	15.06%	17.82%	22.68%	23.17%
31-90 DAYS	Customers	2,612	871	697	1,306	653	620	568	1,179	1,724
	$/Name	$2.76	$5.69	$12.08	$3.95	$9.42	$16.03	$6.07	$14.49	$24.67
	% Response	6.90%	7.59%	9.66%	9.87%	12.56%	12.83%	15.18%	19.32%	19.73%
4-6 MONTHS	Customers	3,811	1,270	1,016	1,906	953	905	828	845	1,057
	$/Name	$2.44	$5.03	$10.68	$3.49	$8.33	$14.17	$5.37	$12.81	$21.81
	% Response	6.10%	6.71%	8.54%	8.72%	11.10%	11.34%	13.42%	17.08%	17.45%
7-9 MONTHS	Customers	3,916	1,305	1,044	1,958	979	930	851	869	1,086
	$/Name	$2.00	$4.13	$8.75	$2.86	$6.83	$11.62	$4.40	$10.50	$17.88
	% Response	5.00%	5.50%	7.00%	7.15%	9.10%	9.30%	11.00%	14.00%	14.30%
10-12 MONTHS	Customers	4,002	1,334	1,067	2,001	1,001	950	870	888	1,110
	$/Name	$1.62	$3.34	$7.09	$2.32	$5.53	$9.41	$3.56	$8.51	$14.48
	% Response	4.05%	4.46%	5.67%	5.79%	7.37%	7.53%	8.91%	11.34%	11.58%
13-18 MONTHS	Customers	7,950	2,650	2,120	3,975	1,988	1,888	1,728	1,764	2,204
	$/Name	$1.24	$2.56	$5.43	$1.77	$4.23	$7.20	$2.73	$6.51	$11.08
	% Response	3.10%	3.41%	4.34%	4.43%	5.64%	5.76%	6.82%	8.68%	8.87%
19-24 MONTHS	Customers	8,120	2,707	2,165	4,060	2,030	1,929	1,765	1,801	2,252
	$/Name	$1.00	$2.06	$4.38	$1.43	$3.41	$5.81	$2.20	$5.25	$8.94
	% Response	2.50%	2.75%	3.50%	3.58%	4.55%	4.65%	5.50%	7.00%	7.15%
25-36 MONTHS	Customers	7,653	2,551	2,041	3,827	1,913	1,818	1,664	2,198	1,622
	$/Name	$0.76	$1.57	$3.33	$1.09	$2.59	$4.42	$1.67	$3.99	$6.79
	% Response	1.90%	2.09%	2.66%	2.72%	3.46%	3.53%	4.18%	5.32%	5.43%
37-48 MONTHS	Customers	15,347	5,116	4,093	7,674	3,837	3,645	3,336	2,404	2,255
	$/Name	$0.48	$0.99	$2.10	$0.69	$1.64	$2.79	$1.06	$2.52	$4.29
	% Response	1.20%	1.32%	1.68%	1.72%	2.18%	2.23%	2.64%	3.36%	3.43%
49-60 MONTHS	Customers	14,391	4,797	3,838	7,196	3,598	3,418	3,128	2,192	1,990
	$/Name	$0.28	$0.58	$1.23	$0.40	$0.96	$1.63	$0.62	$1.47	$2.50
	% Response	0.70%	0.77%	0.98%	1.00%	1.27%	1.30%	1.54%	1.96%	2.00%
60 MONTHS+	Customers	16,302	5,434	4,347	8,151	4,076	3,872	3,544	2,616	2,520
	$/Name	$0.20	$0.42	$0.89	$0.29	$0.70	$1.19	$0.45	$1.07	$1.82
	% Response	0.51%	0.56%	0.71%	0.73%	0.93%	0.95%	1.12%	1.43%	1.46%

A deeper ABT analysis also provides insights about other important customer behaviors. An ABT analysis typically shows that customers purchasing across categories tend to be more profitable and less likely to defect. In business-to-business, ABT commonly reveals that customer companies having multiple (at least two) contacts tended to buy more and be more loyal.

For example, one company with a 65 percent annual attrition rate using ABT found a segment of customers with zero defectors in the prior year. The analysis revealed that customers that purchased at least four times, in four or more product categories, and from two or more contacts, were very likely to be loyal and would remain customers long enough to generate a high lifetime value (LTV).

The results of the ABT analysis could be called simply the *4-4-2 rule* (Four Purchases, Four Products, Two Contacts). Some additional data mining confirmed that any client that met these criteria had a defection rate of zero and a high LTV as well. It took just one slide to present this insight and make a profound impression.

With this insight, the challenge became how to communicate these discoveries to the marketing and sales force in terms they could easily understand, and ABT was born. Everyone intuitively understands the difference between an advocate, a *buyer,* and a tryer.

An overlay using the 4-4-2 rule was prepared and further analysis was done. Each customer was labeled as A, B, or T. Some large customers, with over $1 million in last year's sales, were identified as buyers, since they had only one contact, or bought in only one product category. Their volume made them appear valuable, but they were highly likely to defect.

The sales force then targeted the advocates, many of whom were companies that were previously not targeted. The buyers were hit with a mixture of direct and indirect sales efforts to keep their cost of retention profitable and about 30 percent of the tryers that had a significant chance of becoming a buyer were hit with an indirect sales message.

While the results didn't spin wool into gold, at least, this dot.com survived where many of its peers did not.

What makes ABT especially significant is that it uses as many dimensions as necessary, making the scoring either complex or simple, but always allowing marketers to be able to simplify the output in terms that can be understood. Not all organizations will have something as simple as the 4-4-2 rule, but they might.

All organizations do have advocates, buyers, and tryers. Marketers that sufficiently analyze their behavior so that they can clearly and concisely explain what makes them different and how they can manage marketing efforts based on that knowledge have a clear advantage.

In the end, no matter how complex the process from data analysis to insight is, you still have to simplify and execute the results. In today's world of data overload, especially where customer relationship management (CRM) systems' promises have been found empty, innovating with analyses like ABT and using all the tools in your analytical toolbox, just may be the key to the one true barometer of success—profitability.

4

Quantifying Customer Behavior

Gaining new customers is the lifeblood that keeps a company alive. The challenge is that most organizations spend more on advertising to acquire new customers than they make in profits on the initial sale to those customers. As a result, it costs money to gain new customers.

Lifetime Value

Profits come from making repeat sales to existing customers. Without repeat sales, the money spent trying to attract new customers would never be recovered. When marketers talk about lifetime value, they are really talking about the profits they will earn over time from making repeat sales to customers.

For fundraisers working in non-profits, the situation is often similar. They may be willing to lose money on a promotion to gather new, first-time donors, with the hopes of more than making the loss back with future donations.

For managers trying to understand the business model the question becomes: How much can the organization prudently be spending to attract a customer?

Answering this question will take a step-by-step approach. It can be done using some basic math, combined with information that can be derived from any good marketing database. In addition, it is important to understand the company's capital position and goals for use of capital. That is, how much money does the company have access to for prospecting, and what is the rate of return the company must earn on the money it uses?

Prospecting for new customers or patrons can be viewed as a simple matter of making a financial investment. Money is invested, and time passes before the investment is recovered. Once the investment is recovered, additional income is profit.

For example, the cost of creating and producing a communication effort to turn prospects into customers (or donors) is borne before the first sale from that effort is made. It may be some time before new customers acquired through that effort spend enough to more than cover the initial cost of acquiring them. Over time, in order for the effort to be a success, new customers must spend enough, at a high enough profit margin to more than cover the company's cost of attracting new customers.

The first step in estimating lifetime value is to determine how much it costs to acquire a new customer, i.e., convert a prospect into a customer. For the sake of simplicity, the example will use direct mail, but the same basic methods apply to all media.

(The formula provided below in the Case Study is also provided to you in an Excel file on the CD-ROM that accompanies this book.)

Case Study: Lifetime Value

A company sells a seasonal food product through catalog sales, retail stores, and face-to-face sales. Most (more than 85 percent) of their sales occur during the holidays from mid-November through January.

Most buyers are consumers purchasing either a gift to be sent by the company or for a family gathering. Businesses are not the bulk of the customers, but make up a very large part of the sales. Large business buyers (those who buy for 50 or more employees, for example) are contacted by salespeople. The rest are treated like consumers.

Converting prospects into customers is currently being done near or slightly below break-even level. The best source to acquire new customers above break-even is by marketing to the gift recipients. As the recipients are primarily people receiving the product at their home addresses, most new customers gained this way are consumers.

Converting a business prospect into a buyer is generally done below break-even. That is, acquisition cost tends to be higher for converting business prospects than for converting consumer prospects. However, businesses tend to be much more loyal, place larger orders, and provide more recipients (who can then be acquired).

Recently, the company began acquiring new customers through newspaper advertising. They did this by offering a low-priced selection for $19.95. Their typical average order was $65. While these new buyers are marginally profitable to acquire, they tend to continue to make small orders in the future and are less loyal than buyers that made a larger first order.

Because the business is seasonal and food is perishable, the company will at times use whatever methods are necessary to move inventory, even if it means acquiring customers with a lower lifetime value than would otherwise be possible. Until now, however, they have considered only acquisition cost and have not considered lifetime value.

Compare acquisition cost to lifetime value using the input numbers in Exhibit 4.1a. Also consider value after one year. The company spends most of its prospecting dollars on space advertising, much less reaching consumers, and has virtually discontinued reaching businesses. Would you re-allocate their prospecting dollars, and if so, why?

Use the input numbers in Exhibit 4.1a to compare consumer, business, and space ad acquisition methods. View the results in Exhibit 4.1b or for those using the CD-ROM, select the "Lifetime Value" tab in the Excel workbook, and enter the numbers into the Data Entry Column.

The total cost of the mail piece, including postage, is 70 cents per

Exhibit 4.1a: Consumer, Business, and Space Ad Acquisition Costs

	Consumer Figures:	Business Figures:	Space Ad Figures:
Cost to Reach a Prospect	$0.60	$0.70	$0.01
Average Response	1.10%	0.90%	0.25%
Average Initial Order	$70.00	$80.00	$19.95
Average Repeat Order	$75.00	$110.00	$27.50
Average COGS% (COGS = Cost of Goods Sold)	60.00%	60.00%	70.00%
Cost to Reach a Customer	$0.50	$0.50	$0.50
Number of Customer Contacts/Year	4.0	4.0	4.0
Response per Contact Year One	16.00%	24.00%	8.00%
Response per Contact Year Two	13.00%	16.00%	6.00%
Response per Contact Year Three	11.00%	12.00%	4.00%
Time Value of Money and Risk Factor Discount	20.00%	20.00%	20.00%

piece. (This is the same as 70 cents per reach for media buyers or the same as saying $70 per thousand.) The organization is getting 120 new sales per 1,000 prospects reached, for a 1.2 percent average response.

Given:

- Cost per reach: $0.70 (70 cents)
- Average response: 1.2 percent

Then:

- Cost per reach ÷ Average response = Advertising cost to acquire a customer
- $0.70 ÷ 1.2% (.012) = $58.33

The next step is to determine how much profit margin is earned on the average initial sale. Subtracting this amount from the advertising cost to acquire a customer will determine how much is initially invested in a new customer.

We will assume an average initial order of $75.00 and an average margin of 40 percent, after fulfillment costs, which are the costs of making the sale.

Based on:

- Average initial order: $75.00
- Average margin: 40 percent
- Advertising cost to acquire a customer: $58.33

We find that:

- Average initial order × Average margin = Profit margin on initial sale
- $75.00 × 40% = $30.00
  Advertising cost to acquire a customer – Profit margin on initial sale = Initial investment (per customer)
- $58.33 – 30.00 = $28.33

At this point, the initial investment to acquire a new customer has been determined. In this example, the amount is $28.33. In other words, they lost $28.33 on average for each new customer acquired. Now they need to determine if they will more than make that back in the future.

The next step is to determine likely future profits, and the future cost of marketing to these customers. Customers cannot be re-contacted for free. In addition, to justify the investment, the organization must earn a required rate of investment return, which we will call the *Time Value of Money Discount Factor* (*TVMDF*).

The TVMDF is what we use to recognize the fact that a dollar one, two, or three years from now is not worth as much to us as a dollar today. The TVMDF is based on the rate of return we require on our investment, including what we demand as a result of risk. Using this

Exhibit 4.1b: Lifetime Value

Category	Entry Column	Results Column
Cost to Reach a Prospect	$ 0.75	
Average Response	1.20%	
Advertising Cost to Aquire a Customer		$62.50
Average Initial Order	$75.00	
Average COGS %	60.00%	
Profit on Initial Sale		$30.00
Initial Investment per Customer		$32.50
Cost to Reach a Customer	$ 0.50	
Number of Customer Contacts/Year	4.0	
Annual Marketing Cost		$2.00
Response Rate	Per Contact	Per Year
Year One	16.00%	0.64
Year Two	13.00%	0.52
Year Three	11.00%	0.44
Average Repeat Order	$75.00	
Profit per Customer per Year		
Year One		$17.20
Year Two		$13.60
Year Three		$11.20
Time Value of Money and		
Risk Factor Discount	20.00%	
Future Value of Profit per Customer per Year		
Year One		$14.33
Year Two		$11.33
Year Three		$ 9.33
3 Year Lifetime Value		$ 2.50

factor will give us customer lifetime value, in terms of net present dollars (what future profits are worth to us today). For this example, lifetime value is based on three years' purchases. (The optimal number of years varies from industry to industry, and should be appropriate to each situation.) Certainly, income three years from now is worth less to us today than having the same income today.

In some industries, the formula is not based around a specific time period, but rather a pay-back period, which is the amount of time it takes to recover the initial investment. The management goal in such a case is to make the pay-back period as short as possible. Pay-back period functions as a good way to compare offers for cellular telephone companies, where customers sign long-term contracts. The offers with the shortest pay-back period are making profits sooner and have lower risk.

Managers often set a goal for how long they are willing to wait for new customers to become profitable. Typically, businesses such as catalogs, cellular telephones, and newspapers are willing to wait up to one year to recover their initial investment. In these cases, marketers are really treating a one-year lifetime value as a break-even goal.

To determine at what rate new customers will buy, it is necessary to look at historic data in the data warehouse. How many times customers are re-contacted each year, at what cost, and response rate information must also be gathered.

Assume the organization in this example is mailing four catalogs per year to existing customers, at $0.65 each. This is a lower cost than prospect catalogs, as there is no outside list rental expense. All customer names come out of the house file.

Next to be considered are the response rates of customers during each of the past three years. Note, this is not based on the most recent purchase (recency), it is based on the amount of time since their *first* purchase. That is, people who bought for the first time in the past year have an average response rate, people who bought for the first time two years ago have a different (and usually lower) response rate, and so on. To track lifetime value, it is necessary to track *when* people became customers.

Assume the group of customers who made their first purchase in the past year responds at a rate of 16 percent to each of the four offers. The group of customers who made their first purchase two years ago responds at 13 percent, and the group of three-year customer responds at 11 percent. The numbers drop off, as customers tend to drop off over time, and fewer are recent buyers.

Given:

- 4 contacts per year
- $0.65 average cost per reach
- 16 percent response per contact Year One
- 13 percent response per contact Year Two
- 11 percent response per contact Year Three

Number of contacts × Response per contact = Annual response rate

- Year One: 4 × 16% = 64 percent
- Year Two: 4 × 13% = 52 percent
- Year Three: 4 × 11% = 44 percent

Number of contacts × cost per contact = Annual marketing cost

- 4 × $0.65 = $2.60

Determining the cost per year of reaching an existing customer (the annual marketing cost) and the responses we expect from existing customers (the annual response rate) can simplify the math. Look at each year as if it were a single $2.60 contact, with a 64 percent response rate for one-year customers, 52 percent for two-year customers, and 44 percent for three-year customers.

Note that while we are assuming each contact costs the same and has the same response rate for this example, they often vary tremendously in actual practice. Organizations with many different types of contacts and with different costs per contact, will want to revise the formula to suit their specific needs.

Now it is time to consider TVMDF. Assume this is 20 percent per year (which is the same as paying interest at 20 percent per year to our investors). In other words, if we can achieve 20 percent or greater return, we can attract additional investment. Below 20 percent per year, investors will place their money elsewhere. This amount may be substantially more than the interest rate organizations actually pay banks or investors to cover a risk premium.

The time value of money discount factor for Year One is 1.2, which is the principal (1) plus 20 percent. For Year Two it is 1.44 (1 + 20 percent for two years, or 1.2 squared) and 1.73 for Year Three (1 + 20 percent for three years). This is the opposite of calculating what an investment would be worth with interest since we divide by one plus the interest rather than multiply. This is because we are calculating what a future dollar amount is worth today, not what a dollar amount today will be worth in the future.

It is now necessary to determine the margin on *repeat* sales, which may differ from the margin on *initial* sales if average repeat orders are substantially different than initial orders, but it is calculated the same way.

Given:

- 20 percent Time Value of Money Discount Factor
- $85.00 Average repeat order
- $34.00 Margin on repeat sales (Average repeat order $85.00 × Average margin 40%)
- $2.60 per year marketing cost
- 64 percent response Year One, 52 percent Year Two, and 44 percent Year Three

(Margin on repeat sales × response) − Marketing cost = Profit per year

- ($34.00 × 64 percent) − $2.60 = $19.16 (Year One)

- ($34.00 × 52 percent) – $2.60 = $15.08 (Year Two)
- ($34.00 × 44 percent) – $2.60 = $12.36 (Year Three)

Sum (Profit per year ÷ Time Value of Money Discount Factor) = Present Value Future Profit

- ($19.16 ÷ 1.2) + (15.08 ÷ 1.44) + (12.36 ÷ 1.73) = $33.59

Finally, subtract the Initial Investment to Acquire a Customer from the Present Value of Future Profit to determine if investment goals were met or exceeded.

Given:

- Initial Investment to Acquire a Customer = $28.33
- Present Value of Future Profit = $33.59

Present Value of Future Profit – Initial Investment to Acquire a Customer = Lifetime Return on Investment

- $33.59 – $28.33 = $5.26

In this example, customers were acquired at an almost 50 percent loss on the initial sale, but by the end of the Year Three the organization had recovered their investment, with interest, and is making a profit.

If the sample company could attract investors who would demand less than a 20 percent return, they would be able to expand their prospecting into more marginal lists and still make a profit. This would be particularly wise if by expanding they could lower fixed expenses as a percentage of sales.

On the other hand, if investors view the company as an increasing risk, they may demand more than a 20 percent return on investment. In this case, the company would be forced to prospect more selectively and increase their initial response rates.

Lifetime value calculations show the importance of mining the house file. If the organization does not re-contact its customers as frequently as it should, it cannot achieve the future profits necessary to gather new customers.

If the sample company were to contact customers only three times per year, it would not make a profit. On the other hand, if they could get a similar response rate from each of five contacts per year, they would make more profit and new customers would have a greater lifetime value.

Try these formulas with your own customers. By using this approach, you may be able to determine if you are prospecting too much or too little. You may see how improvements in marketing to existing customers allow you to attract new customers who would otherwise be unprofitable.

Customer Value

An organization's strategic target marketing capabilities can be greatly improved by bringing together the many database tools now at most marketers' disposal into one database. Building a customer value index is a methodology that allows marketers to take immediate advantage of bringing these tools together.

While many corporate leaders are frustrated by a lack of cooperation among the various vertical departments, they seldom see how failing to combine analytical tools such as RFA, lifetime value, and customer segmentation can have a similar effect. Too often, the costs of acquiring a customer are not compared with their follow-up purchases. Sales of support items, such as parts, are sometimes not considered. Follow-up marketing expenses are ignored or considered as the same percentage of sales for all customers and prospects. Customer research, normally done through focus groups and surveys, is seldom used to improve a company's ability to quantify information already available.

There are seven questions that every database marketing driven company strives to answer about all the prospects or customers they can identify. To make each question more realistic, an example answer about a potential customer that is a truck fleet and a truck manufacturer is included. The seven questions are:

1. How much do they/could they buy? (Both from you and from your competitors)

   Consider a trucking company with 100 trucks that trades them in, on average, every five years. This company purchases an average of 20 trucks a year.

2. How likely are they to buy or re-buy from you?

   Assume the trucking company with 100 trucks has 50 cement mixers and 50 dump trucks. Our company manufactures dump trucks, but only 10 percent of the fleets with dump trucks use our product. Our company does not sell any cement mixers. If the trucking company is not a customer already, the likelihood of their buying from our company is probably no higher than 10 percent.

3. If they buy from you, how much are they likely to buy?

   Companies that buy our trucks tend to prefer them. Most of the fleets with our dump trucks are composed of 80 percent or more of our product. So, if we can gain them as a customer, they will probably buy about 40 dump trucks from us over the next five years.

4. If they have a replacement cycle, how long is it?

   Note: This is key to knowing demand. If the same fleet replaced their trucks every ten years, they would buy half as many.

5. Of what they buy from you, how profitable are the sales likely to be?

   For the dump truck manufacturer, larger orders are cheaper to produce, but larger buyers demand higher discounts.

6. How much after-sale support will they demand? (*Both* warranty expense and parts/service sales)

Dump truck buyers are hard on their trucks. Warranty expense is average, since the trucks were designed for this type of service, but replacement part purchases tend to be high. As a result, dump truck customers are more profitable part buyers than most other customers.

7. How much is it likely to cost to sell to this account?

This truck fleet is in a mid-sized city, near a dealer, and large enough for contact by a regional rep. Acquisition cost is likely to be low to average.

Rarely are the answers to these questions found by simply overlaying existing data and comparing it to sales data, especially when new unit data and service support data are held separately. For example, it can be found by overlaying data that one company operates mines and another bottles spring water. While you can quantify the differences in sales by SIC code, what you cannot easily determine is what share of the mining market versus bottling market you control.

Perhaps mining companies use a product almost exclusively, as it is well suited to their needs, while soft-drink bottlers prefer a competitor's product. Also, it may be that since mining operations are dusty and dirty, they purchase more replacement parts and have a shorter replacement cycle. Without doing research to quantify these differences, they will likely be ignored.

Building a customer value index that takes the subtle difference between customers into account can improve a company's ability to target and segment its customer base for maximum profitability.

Customer Value Index

The *customer value index* is based around lifetime value. The three key distinctions between this method and traditional methods are:

1. Customer value index is based on what type of customers they are, while lifetime value tends to be based on source codes, i.e., why customers entered the database.

2. Customer value index tends to be based on all purchases a customer makes from both the company and its competitors. Lifetime value tends to be based on a single department and a single computer system tracked selling process. The purchases from competitors, or capacity to purchase, is typically not part of a lifetime value calculation.

3. Customer value index requires both data from within the company as well as secondary (industry or consumer) data that must be quantified through research, while lifetime value tends to be based only on data from within the company.

A customer value index can show both what customers do buy and what they could buy, based on their likely purchase levels in the product categories being evaluated. As a result, it is both a customer and prospect segmentation tool. Determining the level of product consumed often requires research to quantify information already available about customers and prospects.

One of the first steps in building a customer value index is to assemble all the existing or secondary data about customers and prospects. This includes:

- New unit sales data
- Service and support data
- Results of selling and prospecting campaigns
- Overlay data (either business or consumer)

While it might make for better data, it is usually impractical to survey customers and prospects on a regular basis to gather the marketing information desired. Instead, it is typically more efficient to determine which of the variables about each customer or prospect relates most directly to sales and product usage. This can be done by surveying only a portion of the potential customer universe.

It is through research applied to existing information that variables such as SIC code or age and income can be quantified into actual scores.

For example, in two different SIC codes, companies of equal size may purchase from you, on average, an equal amount. However, through research it can be determined that one SIC code uses five times more of the product than the other, but it is penetrated more heavily by competitors. Research makes it possible to quantify the difference between these groups, and target large potential buyers who otherwise may have been ignored.

In another example, a construction company that builds commercial buildings may use its equipment more heavily than a construction company that builds residential homes. As a result, it may have an average of 75 percent more in replacement parts purchases after the initial sale.

In a third example, it was determined through surveys that buyers of over-the-road refrigerated transport trucks drove over 150,000 miles a year and traded roughly every three years. Buyers of beverage delivery trucks (beer trucks) drove under 50,000 miles a year and traded every ten years. As a result, it was apparent that fleets of similar size were of very dissimilar value depending on how the trucks were used.

The list goes on, but the point is that secondary information by itself does not always answer the questions database marketers have when targeting segmenting customers and prospects.

Once the information is gathered and assumptions checked for reasonableness, all of the components can be gathered into a single index made up of several parts. Normally, two scores are created. First, the actual score is created, based on past purchases for existing customers. Second, the potential score for both customers and prospects based on all the information gathered is created.

It is important to note that the research information is not directly included in each customer or prospect score. Rather, the research is applied to the secondary information. In the previous example where in one SIC code companies consumed five times more than another, the potential sales component of the index would be five times higher for the former SIC code than the latter, assuming all other variables were equal.

The customer value index itself is made up of several scores, which are then strung together much like a regression equation. The separate scoring components typically include:

- Purchase likelihood, usually expressed as a percentage
- Level of purchase, expressed in dollars
- Likely profit margin on unit sales, expressed as a percentage
- Degree of service and replacement parts expected, usually a dollar amount
- Likely profit margin on service and replacement parts, expressed as a percentage
- Likely replacement or life cycle, a score based on the inverse of average life cycle

Put together, the equation looks like:

((Purchase likelihood × Level of purchase × Profit margin) +
(Degree of service × Profit margin)) × (Life cycle score)
= Customer Value Index

Note that the resulting score is actual expected dollars. For an added measure of accuracy, expected marketing expenses can be subtracted from the result. Time value of money can be added to represent the greater value today of more rapid cash flows. Rather than having to convert a meaningless number, actual customer and market potential value can be added directly.

Action Based on a Customer Value Index

An important part of the success of the customer value index is that it be as simple and understandable as possible. By keeping each component score simple, managers can better understand and use the index.

Each component of the index should be designed so each can be used separately, depending on the promotional effort. Salespeople may want to specifically target high potential new unit buyers, while service reps may target heavy parts buyers. Customers in a particular industry may be targeted with a specific campaign.

Targeting customers and prospects based on a customer value index can help target not only the offer, but also the message. Basing messages on the customers and not just on what the organization plans to sell, will provide a better understanding of how offers should be positioned, and which features and benefits are most valued by different market segments.

As knowledge is gained through the use of the customer value index, the accuracy of the component scores can be improved or simply adjusted for a changing marketplace. The score is not an end in itself, but rather should be kept fresh through data updates and periodic research.

While building the index is an often arduous and complex task, once it is done it must appear as a simple, commonsense tool in order for the managers to rely upon it. A score with too many variables or that creates too many segments will be too complicated to use. It is not simply a matter of making the best score, it is a matter of making the best score that is simple enough to understand and use.

It is important to have knowledgeable, experienced marketers and experts who understand the organization assist in the creation of a customer value index, and it is just as important to combine their knowledge with managers who understand the industry as a whole. Rather than being viewed as a computer-modeling tool, creating the customer value index should be viewed as a process to build and use knowledge.

Armed with this knowledge, database marketers can re-direct sales and sales support efforts to the areas with the greatest long-term potential. Product development will have a strong tool to find in which markets their products are perceived as weak and in which they are perceived as strong, so products can be improved or modified for different types of usage. Corporate decision-makers will have a quantifiable means to justify and measure marketing efforts.

A customer value index brings together and improves the tools at a business modeling team's disposal. Very different from a "black box" modeling routine where numbers are fed into a statistical routine and results accepted without explanation, it supplements rather than replaces your knowledge and becomes a part of an organization's strategy.

5
Building Customer Data Files

Every analysis of customer behavior should follow a clear progression: It should proceed from the simple to the more complex. However, simplicity is not defined by the data itself or by the amount of data, but by the *complexity of the data relationships*. Each customer is unique. While a customer may be entered mistakenly into a system more than once or entered into more than one system, they are nevertheless unique.

For example, an organization operates two computer systems, which track:

1. Sales, and is managed by the order entry department (which works under accounting)
2. Contacts, and is managed by the sales department

Every person placing an order or receiving an order can be found in the first database. Every person who interacts with a salesperson, whether it be to gather technical information, negotiate sales terms, or request promotional materials such as a free hat with the company's logo, can be found in the second database.

A customer easily could be entered in several places in a database. For example, the same person could be listed as a bill-to and as a ship-to in the first system. They also could have been entered into the second system by more than one salesperson. In addition, this individual could be entered differently in both systems, causing further duplication.

When this is the case, a simple question such as "How many customers do we have?" becomes very difficult to answer. If a person can be listed in three or four places in the database that contains 40,000 total customer listings, how many unique customers does that company really have: 40,000 or only 10,000? If a company's sales are $4,000,000 a year, does the average customer spend $100 a year or $400 a year?

Before any credible analysis can proceed, duplicate customer entries first must be found, matched, and made unique.

The Progression of an Analysis

To create an analysis, we need to proceed in a step-wise fashion:

1. Step One: Match duplicates among customers and prospects so that each customer can be found uniquely in the data.
2. Step Two: Understand the customers and transactions.
3. Step Three: Understand what customers buy.
4. Step Four: Understand what an items cost.

The first and simplest step in creating your analysis is to match duplicates among customers and prospects so each customer can be found "uniquely" in the data. Determining what makes two customer entries a unique match can be very difficult. A customer could be a single person, a household (family) at a single address, a company (with one or more contact individuals), and so on.

Defining who or what is the unique customer is the key requirement for understanding customer behavior. If we cannot tell if someone is making three purchases or if three people are each making one purchase, we will learn very little about each customer.

Consider the following example where an organization has the following customers:

- Record 1: ABC Electrical, 100 Carriage Center, Chicago, IL, 60101
- Record 2: Henry Gibson, PO Box 200, 100 Carriage Center, Chicago, IL, 60101
- Record 3: ABC Electrical, PO Box 200, Chicago, IL, 60101

Are there three customers or only one? Without reviewing the data, there are three records. Upon close inspection, we can see there is only one customer. Now, let's assume that the first record (tryer one) matched to annual sales of $750. The second (buyer one) matched to annual sales of $5,750, and the third (buyer two) matched to annual sales of $3,500. Consider Exhibit 5.1.

Exhibit 5.1: Three Buyers or One Advocate?

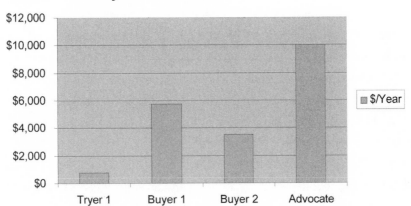

For a marketer that does not combine matching customer listings into unique customers, there appears to be one tryer and two buyers.

However, if they are properly combined, it is clear there is only one advocate. Simply relying on de-duplication will not be sufficient, as none of the duplicate records are advocates by themselves, and any of three records could be kept while the others are dropped. Simple de-duplication easily could lead to treating this advocate like a tryer. Treating this customer like an advocate, with communications and offers relevant to an advocate, will be far more effective and efficient than simply duplicating communications and offers intended for tryers and buyers.

The next step in the process of creating an analysis is to understand the customers and their transactions. The data relationships are complex because one customer can make many transactions. In addition, the transactions themselves must be recorded accurately in the database in order to be useful.

For example, if a customer were entered in the database twice and had made two purchases, it would appear as though two customers each made one purchase. When customers are identified uniquely, we can then accurately apply transactions, i.e., who spent how much on which day.

Transactions themselves are a challenge to understand. For example, a company selling hams to businesses for employee and client gifts tracks all ham sales in one system, along with smaller gift certificate sales. The home office handles large gift certificate sales. As a result, roughly 20 percent of their sales are not in the main transactional system. Without tracking these home office sales in the same system, many customers' purchases are greatly understated.

Each transaction must correspond to a customer. Orphan transactions (transactions that do not correspond to any customer) cannot be used to properly classify tryers, buyers, and advocates. These transactions typically signal a problem with missing data and must be corrected before further analysis can proceed.

Transaction amounts are often misunderstood as well. For example, a company may show gross annual sales of $12,500,000, net annual sales of $12,000,000, and net sales including shipping of $13,000,000. Which is it? Marketers must know which amount corresponds to the organization's sales or how to determine what corresponds. Generally, marketers consider net sales (without shipping) as the "correct" amount, but this is not always so. Analyses are commonly wrong simply because the wrong amount column was used for sales figures. Analysts working with transactions must be vigilant about using the correct amount column.

Once transactions are correctly recorded and correctly understood, they can be properly combined with customer data. After this is done, and we have determined who buys how much and how frequently they buy, it is possible to proceed to the next level of complexity.

The third step in the process is understanding what customers buy. In order to know who is buying what, we must know who each customer is and which transactions they have made. Then, we can understand which items they bought in each transaction.

When a customer makes a transaction, they can purchase several different things, which adds another layer of complexity to the analysis. For example, a transaction at a hardware store could include a wrench, nuts, bolts, and washers. Wrenches, nuts, bolts, and washers are four unique items. In addition, the items are probably in more than one product category. The wrench is a tool, while the nuts, bolts, and washers are fasteners.

As a general rule, marketers sell far more items than they imagine. Marketers who think they sell dozens of unique items sell hundreds; marketers who think they sell hundreds, sell thousands. Categorizing items helps to group and simplify them, making it much easier for marketers to manage.

Usually, items are categorized from the organization's perspective, and not that of the customer. For example, a seller of collectable coins had one product category for over 90 percent of the items they sold. It was simply "coin." However, they sold all kinds of coins: Roman coins, gold coins from shipwrecks, Civil War coins, painted coins, and so on. Categorizing the coins to correlate with the various interests of the buyers made it much easier to segment communication based on what people bought.

The last step in creating an analysis is understanding what items cost. In order to know how profitable customers are, it is necessary to understand what it costs to deliver what it is we are selling to customers. Though this sounds simple to determine, it is, in fact, complex.

Most accounting and management systems are designed to measure product costs in bulk. For example, one manufacturer assigned cost-of-goods sold based on the plant where each item was produced. All the products from any given plant had the same cost-of-goods sold as a percentage of the sale price. For a company-wide, year-to-year total profit margin, that method works fine. It does not work on a product-by-product, customer-by-customer basis. The same product sold for $50 by one salesperson with a 40 percent profit margin might be sold by another salesperson for $100, again with a 40 percent profit margin. In the first case, the cost-of-goods sold would be $20, in the second case, the cost-of-goods sold for exactly the same product is $40. In addition, a plant may have a high margin item they make very cheaply and a low margin item that is difficult to produce. Both would be given the same cost-of-goods sold percentage.

In another example, in consulting for the CEO of a company, we found they didn't have accurate costs on a product-by-product basis. We prepared several overall profit margin assumptions based on a different overall cost-of-goods sold percentage. The CEO looked at the assumptions, said the 40 percent number was close and to use that as the cost-of-goods sold for all products.

In both examples, the assumption is that the margin is the same for all items, making it impossible to tell which customers are more profitable than others. It does not matter what they buy or don't buy, their profitability appears the same. In reality, some customers demand higher discounts than others, some buy higher margin items than others, and largest customers are often quite different from highest margin customers. Without accurate item-by-item costs, it is impossible to be sure which customers are most profitable.

Merge/Purge Is the Foundation

Once we have completed our initial data collection, it is time to begin cleaning the database. *Merge/Purge*, the direct marketing term for finding, matching, and eliminating duplicate customers and prospects, is the foundation of all customer data analysis. Without it, accurate analysis is not possible and sophisticated statistical tools are worthless.

Merge logic is the set of rules an organization uses to find, match, and eliminate duplicate customers and prospects. Merge logic is something that can, and in many cases should be, custom-designed for each organization. Here is what several types of "typical" merge logic use to find matches:

- Consumer Direct Mail: Zip or Postal Code, Street Number, Street Name, Last Name. Note, while some do not use last name (only address) this is problematic in apartments and high rises. While some logics include apartment numbers, most do not, and people often leave apartment numbers off their address, causing even more problems.

- Consumer Telephone: Direct-mail logic PLUS one or more phone numbers. Since people can have more than one phone line, any match of address OR phone is a match.

- Business-to-Business Direct Mail: Zip or Postal Code, Street Number, Street Name, *or* P.O. Box Number instead of street information. Some logics will use company name instead of or in addition to street information. However, if a business at one address has two names, such as Darrel Erickson Buick and Darrel Erickson GMC Truck, it can cause a duplicate mailing. If a company has many locations in a single Zip Code, as is common with realtors, it can cause many names to be duped out (dropped) by mistake.

- Business-to-Business Sales: Duns number (a company identifier created by Dun & Bradstreet [D&B], a business data compiler) can be used to identify company locations and tie together headquarters with subsidiary locations. For example, all the Buick dealers in the United States could be linked together using this information from Dun & Bradstreet.

  However, business relationships can be very complex, and even D&B data is not 100 percent accurate. In many lines of business, matches using compiled data often find less than 50 percent of the target. In such cases, custom matches on company name, government identifications, such as Department of Transportation (DOT) number, unknown ship-to addresses attached to known ship-to addresses, or matches on contacts who show up in more than one location can be useful. Generally, some trial-and-error is needed to get it right.

- Business Contacts: Occasionally contacts are listed in the database separately, and no tag is created to tie them to their company. In such a case, it is necessary to tie each person to his or her company location (similar to Business-to-Business Direct Mail logic) while making sure each person is listed only once (similar to Consumer Direct Mail logic).

As a manager buying merge/purge services, expect merge/purge logic to be oversold, especially if it is off-the-shelf. While many business-to-consumer direct mailers can utilize canned logic, most other business can benefit from creating a logic that best fits their own needs. Expect to go through several versions of logic before finding the best overall fit for your needs.

Data Checks

Before performing any analytical work on any data, it is important to make sure the data is complete and accurate. This is the *data check* phase and it is crucial to the success of your analysis.

The data check phase not only assures that data are correct; it helps refine the scope of the project if you did not realize how big (or small) it was. For example, an organization thought they had a simple database project, since they had 40 field salespeople and about 6,000 customers and sold only a few hundred different items. Upon receipt of the data, we found they had 25,000 customers, sold over 5,000 items, and had hundreds of thousands of transactions per year. In addition, most items had $0.00 in the cost field. Simply loading the data and taking a quick look at it proved the project was many times larger than had been imagined.

Items that need to be checked include:

- Number of customers (before and after merge/purge)
- Number of prospects (before and after merge/purge)
- Sales (in total and by time period from transactions)
- Number of items actually sold (from transactions)
- Number of items available (from product files)
- Number of customers making a transaction
- Orphan records

Orphan records are data records that do not tie to records in other tables (files) as they should. For example, a transaction that does not tie to a customer is an orphan transaction. Usually, the presence of orphan records indicates some data is missing.

Total sales by time period is important to check, to make sure transactions and sales are understood properly. For example, if a company measures sales by weekly periods, and four weeks equals a month, sales from the four June weekly periods will not match sales from June 1st through the 30th. In such a case, a "sales month" does not begin on the 1st and end on the 30th or 31st. If "June" began on the second it will end on the 29th.

Usually, the data check reveals data are missing, which allows you to collect the missing data before you begin your analysis. Nobody wants to present an analysis based on $10 million in sales only to have everyone then point out sales were $20 million.

Relational Versus Flat Databases

Relational databases are made up of several tables (files) that relate to one another by key fields, such as a unique customer ID, transaction number, product ID (SKU), and so on. Data are typically gathered and stored in relational databases. Accounting systems, order entry systems, and production management systems are all examples of systems based on a relational database.

A *flat* or *flat-file database* is only one file. Unlike a relational database, which can represent one-to-many relationships (such as one customer having many transactions), a flat database represents one-to-one relationships only.

While working systems, such as accounting systems, order entry systems, and production management systems are relational databases, analytical systems, such as SAS or SPSS, perform analytical work primarily with flat databases. This is important to remember since how data are moved from relational databases to a flat database materially affects the outcome of an analysis.

In order to move data from a relational to a flat database, the data must be summarized. A customer with ten transactions totaling $750 cannot be shown ten times in the flat database, but can be shown with ten transactions in the relational database. Instead, the customer is shown with a count of ten in a transaction frequency field (column).

The analyst may choose to simply show one amount ($750) and one count of transactions (ten) for this customer. However, a customer making ten transactions over five years and a customer making ten transactions over five months are quite different. By the same token, a customer spending $660 on their first purchase and making nine purchases of $10 each is quite different than a customer making ten purchases of $75 each.

The analyst could choose to show or not show a total of purchases and purchases by time period. The choices of how to represent the data for analysis are based on both the analyst's understanding of the analytical software and the analyst's understanding of the data. The better the analyst understands the data, the better the analysis.

Keep in mind that analysts start with data and end up with statistics. Which data are included, which data are excluded, and how that data are represented are all up to the analyst. Before you accept the statistical output as fact, bear in mind it went through some degree of interpretation by an analyst.

Data Format Versus Data Content

Data stored in different formats or from systems that use different software languages can be analyzed using a common system. However, an extra step is required to bring the data into a common format or language.

While translating data to a common format or language can be difficult or impossible, translating data formats is quite common.

Translating English data into Arabic data without losing or changing any meaning may be difficult, but translating Excel format into Access format is quite easy. Still, data formats do not translate themselves. If a team uses a common format, it reduces or eliminates time spent interpreting files, adjusting format, importing, exporting, and so on. Finding the lowest common denominator format that works with all or as many systems as possible is a huge time-saver.

Most software that can be used to analyze data can read or at least import and export data in many formats. SPSS, SAS, Oracle, Access, Excel, and FoxPro all have this capability, to name only a few. As much as possible, avoid any database or analytical system that exclusively uses a proprietary data format (a data format unique to that product). This serves no one, except maybe the software vendor, and causes problems when information is needed on other systems.

For example, some databases like Access allow long field names. Some databases like FoxPro limit field names to ten characters, while others, like SPSS, limit field names to eight characters. If you know you will analyze the data in SPSS, you may as well limit field names to eight characters, whether you plan to use Access or FoxPro with the data initially.

Data collection usually requires some data translation. This is because the software used to collect and manage the data in the production systems is different than the software used to move and manipulate data for an analysis, which is different from the statistical modeling software that will ultimately be used for complex analysis.

Expect to move data from one format to another in the course of any analysis. It is the data content that is most crucial.

Different Data Sources Equal Different Data Meanings

Just as data may need to be translated from one format to another, data content may need to be translated as well. Before data can be combined from separate sources, some degree of data checking and analysis must be done with data from each system.

For example, one system may show sales with shipping in one field, while another may show sales and shipping amounts separately. One system may show sales as occurring the day the order was made, another may show the sale as the day it was shipped, and a third may show sales as the day the payment was received. In order for that kind of data to be combined into a flat database and have equal meaning, some kind of translation must occur.

International data commonly require translation. Comparing sales in U.S. dollars to sales in Canadian dollars isn't apples to apples. A common unit should be selected and one or all sales changed to be in that unit.

Expect to spend some time on data translation. It is well worth another data check phase whenever data is combined or compared across systems to spot obvious inconsistencies.

Realistic Time Frames

Data checks, converting data formats, and translating data consume most of the time involved in building a database to analyze. Rarely does the actual analysis take one-half or even one-quarter of the time required for the entire analysis. The size and complexity of the organization has a direct impact on how long it will take to gather, correct, and understand data prior to any real analysis. Since there can be so much variation, following are some examples of how long projects have taken for these early phases.

Case Study: Business-to-Business Medical Equipment Manufacturer

This organization has about 10,000 active customers, sold several thousand different items, and did about half a billion dollars a year in sales. They are a division of a larger manufacturing firm.

Initially, they thought they would need to build a small and simple database. For example, the president assumed sales reps entered all their own sales, and with 50 sales reps, how many transactions could there be?

Instead, what they found was:

- Their 10,000 customers were mixed in with 250,000 customers from other divisions and had to be broken out separately—no easy task.
- They had millions of transactions. If the sales reps had entered them, they would each have made and entered a sale every three minutes. Clearly, a large volume of orders were made another way.
- Costs were not accurate among thousands of items.
- Reps were not assigned to the right customers in many cases.
- Product categories were missing or inaccurate.

It took about nine months and $150,000 in extra effort to get the data accurate and consistent enough to be useful. All told, the project cost about five times what was originally estimated.

Their effort to build a small and simple database was hampered by two things:

1. The managers did not realize how much data they had. They greatly underestimated how many customers, transactions, and products they actually sold.

2. Nobody was aware that data were incomplete or incorrect in so many areas. The data they had had been sufficient to run the reports they were used to, but it was insufficient to create the reports they desired.

Fortunately, it is usually cheap and easy to find out before beginning the project if the underlying data will support higher analytics. Unfortunately, most organizations commit to and begin projects before determining if they have the right data to succeed.

Case Study: Consumer Cataloger

A consumer cataloger with a 144-page catalog selling thousands of pet care products wanted to understand how profitable each product was in relation to the amount of space each product was given in the catalog. This type of advertising space analysis is common for catalogers and is called a *Square Inch Report.*

The initial report took about two days to create. However, upon reviewing it, their in-house accountant realized the item-by-item costs in the catalog system were not accurate. It should be noted their accounting and catalog systems were separate, which is not uncommon. In addition, some of the product costs in the accounting system were not current.

With thousands of items, it took the company six months to go through each product listing, assure that the costs were accurate, and set up a system to keep costs accurate.

When they were done with this work, the report was produced in about two hours.

Rapid Development Approach

Many organizations go down a path of building a large database (usually a *customer relationship management [CRM] system*) with a large price tag, which they hope to implement all at once. Most fail. Sometimes the projects are abandoned. Sometimes they end up with an expensive data black hole that collects information no one uses.

There are several rules that should be followed to ensure success when building a database to better understand customer behavior. They include:

- If you can't do it manually, you can't automate it. Until you know what it is you are trying to accomplish, and can do it on a small scale, no one can create a computer program to do it for you.
- Data checking is the largest, slowest, and hardest part of the process. It must be done *before* a new system is rolled out. Failure to do a thorough data check results in faulty data that produce incorrect reports.
- Until the relationships with customers, including who are advocates, buyers, and tryers, are understood, it is difficult, if not impossible, to build a system to effectively monitor and support strategy. It does not make sense to build a system to support a certain strategy when that strategy is still an unknown.
- The task of building better databases is more a challenge of human resources and knowledge allocation than of capital allocation. Trying to spend your way out of a database problem is a sure recipe for disaster. It is like trying to dig out of a hole.
- When the promise of "we'll have a new system that will answer all our questions" proves to be false, people stop (or never start) using the new system.

The *rapid development approach* is a start-from-where-you-stand method, not unlike a skunkworks approach. Data are first gathered, checked, and manipulated on inexpensive, flexible systems. As more knowledge is gathered about customers and prospects, necessary functions that are being done manually can be automated.

The data check phase never really ends, it just changes as reports become more sophisticated and the rapid development approach allows potentially expensive and embarrassing mistakes to be caught before they are rolled out.

In the long run, a small team with a small budget that produces results as they go is more likely to be successful than a large team with a large budget that plans to deliver a complete system all at once.

Building a Contact Strategy

There is an old database-marketing axiom—the 40/40/20 rule—that states that the success of a campaign depends 40 percent on the list, 40 percent on the offer, and 20 percent on the creative. According to this view, a marketer's database, i.e., their list, drives 40 percent of a campaign's success. Marketers who are on the cutting-edge understand that their database also supports their offer selection and even their creative. How? Segmentation.

Segmentation is a generic term that describes any way marketers may divide the marketplace in order to reach different groups or targets with different messages. Simply put, proper segmentation allows you to create offers and select or de-select names very efficiently. When using a database to create segments, each segment should describe at least two things:

1. What makes the segment unique? A marketer must understand how the unique characteristics of the segment are likely to respond to certain offers.

2. How likely is the segment to respond? A marketer needs to decide whether or not and when and how often to contact that segment.

For many marketers, state-of-the-art segmentation means using the database to determine with the greatest possible accuracy which customers will or will not respond to a given offer. They may point with pride to a statistical technique that will select the best 20,000 names from the database. But how did they decide to reach 20,000 people? Will knowledge from the statistical technique help the marketer create more effective offers? Or is it simply a Go/No-Go name selection tool?

For data-driven segmentation techniques to focus solely on predicting responses and sales misses the point of database marketing entirely. Database marketers are not trying to just *predict* customer behavior, they are trying to *change* customer behavior. Managing change requires understanding, which is why proper segmentation must support proper understanding.

Segmentation Is Tactical; Marketing Is Strategic

Using statistical techniques to segment customers is an effective tactic, but how and when those segments are used is strategic. While there is no doubt that segmentation can be a very effective tactic, it can be more effective when employed as part of an overall strategy.

For example, consider the two following scenarios for a database marketing organization that has a database with 100,000 names.

Scenario One: The marketing manager has 20,000 mail pieces ready for a September campaign and asks the statistician to select the best 20,000 names. He does so using an advanced, statistical technique that has been repeatedly shown to be highly predictive of who will respond.

The 20,000 pieces are identical and each customer will get the same offer. The offer, which is $20 off any order over $100, has been the most effective overall in the past.

The mail pieces go out, and the campaign is a success. Responses are very close to what was predicted, and all segments within the 20,000 pieces perform above break-even.

Scenario Two: The marketing manager is planning a September campaign. She sits down with the statistician and reviews past campaigns, current customer segments, and past offer performance.

They realize that September has been a strong month in the past and they estimate they can reach 40,000 customers profitably. They also found customers with lower average orders tended not to respond well to their best-performing overall offer, which is $20 off any order over $100, and customers with very high average orders often placed smaller orders than usual when given that offer.

They create 40,000 mail pieces that can be versioned for three different offers. Customers with low average orders get $10 off any order over $50, typical customers get $20 off any order over $100, and customers with very large average orders get $100 off any order over $500.

The mail pieces go out, and the campaign is a success. All segments within the 40,000 pieces perform at or above break-even. Furthermore, the low average order segment had a higher average order than usual, with most spending over $50. The high average order segment had a much higher average order than usual as well. Interestingly, response rates were better than expected in the low average order segment, and about the same in the high average order segment, despite the increase in average order.

Exhibit 6.1: Performance by Segment

Performance by segment, shown as sales per customer contacted ($ per name):

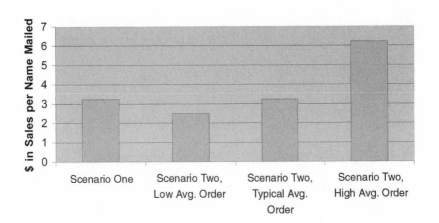

Now that you have read both scenarios, you can see which one presents the more advanced use of the database. In scenario two, the manager used the database segmentation strategically. She found not only a larger audience, but she tailored her communication for each of the three segments. She increased sales in segments that otherwise would have been treated the same with proper offer selection and she increased sales overall by finding more profitable names to contact.

Exhibit 6.2: Overall Sales by Segment
Overall sales is shown here:

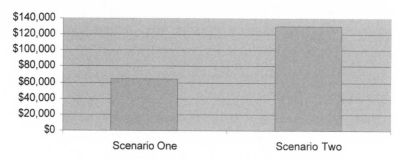

Segmentation by Frequency of Contact

For many organizations, business is seasonal. While they may contact customers year-round, they may prospect in only one season or even one month. Would there be an advantage for such companies to prospect more frequently? What can segmentation analysis tell them about their customer base?

Consider the following example. A company selling soaps, lotions, and candles by catalog contacted customers and prospects mainly around the holidays. They had been in business for about five years and most customers were one-time buyers. Upon reviewing their database, they discovered that new customers were as likely to buy again, regardless of the time of year, if they received a new catalog. The big difference was in recency. Customers who didn't get a catalog for several months were not as likely to buy again as customers who happened to have bought shortly before the next catalog was mailed.

As a result, the company changed their communication strategy. Catalogs now go out ten times a year, even though some mailings are quite small. For example, for some mailings, only buyers from the last 90 days are chosen, for others, during peak season, buyers who hadn't purchased for several years may be contacted. With no other changes, the number of three-time plus buyers doubled in less than a year, repeat purchases soared, and lifetime value jumped dramatically.

Exhibit 6.3 shows the quantity of catalogs that were sent out before the analysis and the monthly sales from those catalogs.

Exhibit 6.3: Pre-Segmentation Analysis Catalog/Sales Correlation

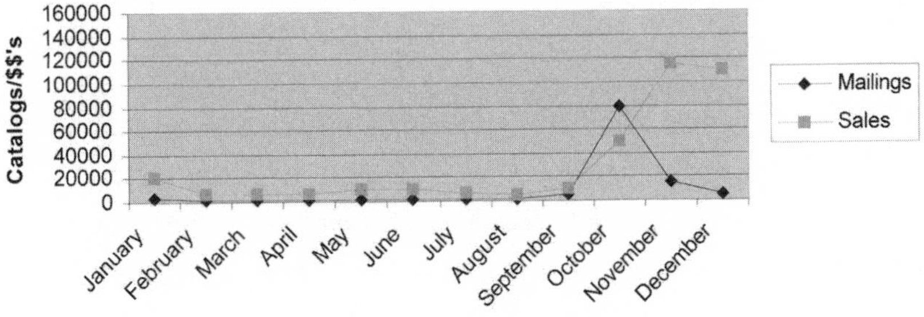

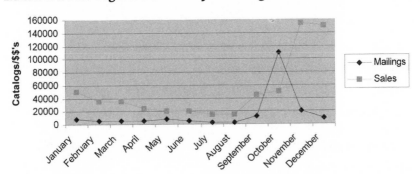

Exhibit 6.4 shows the quantity of catalogs mailed after the analysis and the monthly sales from those catalogs.

Exhibit 6.4: Post-Segmentation Analysis Catalog/Sales Correlation

Notice that sales were much stronger over the year, with monthly sales rarely below $20,000. The curves look similar, but in fact, annual sales nearly doubled and the increased repeat sales allowed the company to increase prospecting efforts during the holiday sales season. By making customers worth more, that made prospecting more valuable.

The segmentation analysis performed by this company didn't merely change the tactics or the schedule for when various customers received their mailings. It changed the company's strategy. Before, they thought of themselves as a holiday/seasonal business, driven mainly by gift-giving. Now, they know their best customers buy again and again for themselves. If they don't contact their customers often enough, they will lose them. This new strategy changed the tone and timing of the offers and changed the creative message.

Understanding House File Segmentation

Being able to contact customers with different needs, in different ways, requires what is called *house file segmentation*. The term "house file" is a marketing term that means "any customer or prospect data that come from within the organization." A customer list is part of the house file, as are names gathered at a trade show. A rented list of names used for a single mailing is not part of the house file.

House file segmentation fits into a strategy to grow the customer base, increase loyalty, and grow share of customers. In some ways it drives the strategy, in other ways it reflects the strategy. For example, an organization whose goal is trying to grow rapidly would look more at lifetime value and future potential sales than an organization whose goal is to maximize cash flow today.

Using the database to create effective house file segmentation should help marketers answer basic questions such as:

- Who should be contacted?
- What makes segments different?

- What offers are likely to be appropriate?
- Which customers are likely to be most valuable?
- When should contacts be made?
- Where do the best customers come from?
- Which media are most effective in making contacts?

There are several components for each of these questions. Following is a guide to these components.

Who Should Be Contacted?

In order to know who should be contacted, it is necessary to predict three basic behaviors:

1. How likely is someone to respond?
2. If they respond, how much are they likely to spend?
3. Are they likely to continue to respond in the future?

As a general rule, dollar value/name, or how much was sold on average to each name contacted, is a more effective business measure than response rate alone. It is a combination of the first two behaviors noted above, and marketers who measure results both by response rate and dollar value/name tend to rely more heavily on dollar value/name.

Consider the following example. An organization tests two different promotions. Promotion A goes to 20,000 people and gets a 2.5 percent response. Promotion B goes to 10,000 people and gets a 1.5 percent response. Promotion A has $15,000 in total sales, while promotion B has $12,500 in sales. Which promotion was more effective?

	Contacts	Responses	Response %	Sales	$/Name
Promotion A	20,000	500	2.50%	$15,000	$0.75
Promotion B	10,000	150	1.50%	$12,500	$1.25
Overall	30,000	650	2.17%	$27,500	$0.92

While promotion A did have the higher response rate, promotion B was more effective financially. Promotion B gathered $1.25 in sales for every name mailed, while promotion A gathered only 75 cents. Had promotion A performed as well as promotion B, sales would have increased by $10,000.

Few circumstances exist where a lower dollar value/name to a similar audience is better. The exception is if future sales are likely to be high, simply getting more customers to buy for the first time *may* be a more effective strategy. A clear understanding of lifetime value is required to target customers and potential customers that may not be short-term winners, but who could pay off in the long run, even though response rates and dollar value/name look sub-par in the short run. Most organizations attempting to gather new customers are hampered by weak retention. Because they don't do a good job of keeping existing customers, new customers are not as valuable to them as they could be, so they cannot afford to spend as much attracting new customers. If they did a better job on retention, their challenges with prospecting problems would be greatly reduced.

What Makes Segments Different?

It is not enough to segment customers based on total spending. There are nearly always specific customer behaviors that correlate with spending or loyalty and marketers need to understand which triggers are most effective. Each difference in the customer's behavior should lead to a different response by the organization. How each customer responded should move them into a different segment.

Some typical differences include:

- **Average Order.** Some customers make a lot of small purchases; some make a few large purchases. In general, average order is a more effective segmentation tool than total "monetary" (overall spending). Recency-frequency-average (RFA) order segmentation will nearly always be substantially more effective than a recency-frequency-monetary (RFM) segmentation.

A retail jeweler segmenting customers based on RFM changed to RFA, and targeted offers near or just above customer's average order. For example, a segment of frequent purchasers of small items had previously been treated like large purchasers, since they had a high overall monetary. They had responded so poorly to the high-dollar offers they had received in the past, the "no offer" control group often beat the group getting promotions. Simply fitting the offer to typical purchase behavior segments increased average spending by nearly 20 percent.

- **One Item vs. Many.** In general, the greater the variety customers buy, the greater the likelihood they are to return. By contrast, a large customer that buys only one item often has a high likelihood of defecting.

  A wholesale manufacturer of scented candles found that the retailers who sold the most and remained customers over time tended to buy (and offer) the full line of candles. Retailers who sold only a few scents, even if they made several large orders, tended to drop the candles after some time. Simply offering promotions to the retailers that encouraged to purchase all the scents in the product line greatly reduced attrition.

- **Time on File.** New customers often behave differently than customers who are set in a pattern. New customers often try many different things and are ripe prospects for cross selling.

  A symphony had been targeting offers to patrons based on what performances they had attended in the past. Upon reviewing the data, they found new patrons (people who had been with them two years or less) tended to sample many different events. After that, they tended to settle into what they enjoyed the most. As a result, the symphony changed offers to new patrons to cover a variety of events, increasing not only sales, but also retention.

- **Multiple Contacts.** Business customers buying with more than one contact person tend to be both more loyal and to purchase more than customers with only one contact. Component manufacturers (makers of parts that go into finished goods, like switches, lights, and so on) typically find they need at least one contact per specific area, such as engineering, production, purchasing, and design.

  A company selling business supplies found that not only were customers with more than one contact more loyal, they found that customers with two contacts, bought, on the average, more than twice as much as customers with one contact, and that customers with three contacts bought more than three times as much, and so on. Apparently, if more than one contact was making purchases, they felt more comfortable buying from that supplier than if they were the only one in the office who bought from them.

- **Family Size.** Buyers of many consumer goods, such as milk, detergent, socks, and so on, range across the spectrum of age and lifestyles. For many of these purchases, the best customer is often in their thirties or forties, though in actuality age has little to do with it. For most typical goods, the driving factor in how much people buy is family size.

  A portrait studio company profiled their customers and found parents of children under the age of two were their best customers. However, age was more offset by number of children in the family. A family with a four-year-old and a six-year-old tended to be more valuable than a family with one newborn. Consider how the average sale looks by age vs. number of children:

Exhibit 6.5: Average Annual Sales by Child's Age

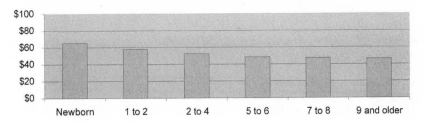

Exhibit 6.6: Average Annual Sales by Number of Children

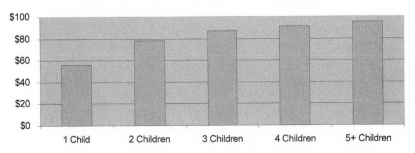

As you can see, while age of children is important, the number of children (i.e., family size) is even more important: More kids, more pictures!

- **Active vs. Inactive Donors.** Many non-profits consider active donors to be people who have given in the past year or two. However, viewing active donors as people who do something in addition to donating can be just as powerful.

A major university studied its alumni in order to determine which demographic factors were most important in finding new donors for the alumni association. They found age, income, and family situation had little effect. What they did find was whether or not someone had volunteered, been on a committee, or attended a function was highly correlated with becoming a giver. A donor that is active in the association was far more likely to become (or remain) a donor than one who was not!

What Offers Are Likely to Be Appropriate?

Constructing offers that are appropriate for each segment requires understanding the unique needs and behaviors of those segments. Some of this understanding comes from (or is validated by) testing these offers. Testing should be able to help answer questions such as the following:

- Is average order substantially different among segments? If so, should buyers who have been spending $50 with each purchase get a different offer than buyers who have been spending $500 with each purchase?

  A jeweler tested $100 off purchases of $500 or more against $25 off purchases of $100 or more in two segments: (1) people who had spent over $500 in the past, and (2) people who had spent under $100 in the past. In addition, they held out a test group that received no offer. They found the $500 buyers reacted best to the $100 off $500 offer, and reacted so poorly to $25 off $100 that the "no offer" group actually responded better. Similarly, $100 buyers responded best to $25 off $100, and the "no offer" group actually out-performed the $100 off $500 test group. Clearly, offers based around average order were highly effective.

- Are different segments buying different things? In other words, are best buyers simply buying expensive items and "average" buyers purchasing cheaper items?

  A manufacturer of woodworking equipment made two

kinds of machines: (1) a relatively inexpensive saw used by hobbyists and (2) a relatively expensive commercial machine used by businesses. Based on average order, the buyers of expensive machines were always best customers. In reality, there were two different markets, each with its own tryers, buyers, and advocates. Segmenting both buyers with the same criteria simply confused marketing strategy. Separating the hobbyists from the commercial market before further segmentation proved more logical and effective.

- Are different segments buying more types of things, while some buy only one or two things? In general, customers who buy a greater variety of things are more valuable and more loyal.

  A business-to-business seller found customers buying in multiple categories were highly loyal, while those who cherry-picked only a single item were highly likely to leave. They then found they had customers spending over a million dollars with them on one and only one item. Based on RFA, these customers looked great, but selling them different items proved to be the key to improving their loyalty.

Which Customers Are Likely to Be Most Valuable?

Understanding which customers have potential to become more valuable helps you understand how to most effectively grow loyalty within your house file. Here are some tips to help you spot a target (even if their purchase behavior makes them a small customer) to move up to a more valuable segment:

- Does the customer look like or share characteristics of a best customer in terms of demographics (or firm profile in business-to-business sales)?

  A manufacturer of truck engines found that many large truck fleets had a few trucks with their engines, but many trucks with their competitors' engines. Based on past sales, these fleets appeared to be small customers. However, the manufacturer found that by targeting these fleets to increase their share they could greatly increase sales and turn a small account into a major customer.

- If they are buying only one or a few items, could they be sold a greater variety of items?

  An office buying large amounts of copy paper almost certainly has many copiers, uses a lot of toner, and consumes many office supplies. Large purchases of a single item commonly used in tandem with other items is a tip-off that a customer could buy a great deal more.

- If there is only one contact name or no contact name (not unusual in business-to-business) would reaching more people in the organization increase sales potential?

  Having more than one contact may be necessary for success. It may be necessary to contact the person who needs the product, the person who approves the purchase of the product, and the person who actually makes the purchase. In addition, multiple contacts is a hedge against employee turnover. Databases that include blank contact name fields or list only department titles such as "Accounts Payable" are a clear indication that better data are needed, which could translate into better sales.

  Similar logic can be applied to prospects. It is important to first define where profitable customers come from and what they look like, rather than simply targeting markets because they are large or easy to reach.

When Should Contacts Be Made?

The best timing and frequency of offers often varies substantially among segments. To know when to test, you need to know the following:

- How seasonal is the market by segment? Typically, season-ality takes on two components that marketers often ignore. Best customers tend to buy more regularly and often less seasonally than occasional customers or first-time buyers. Consider the chart in Exhibit 6.7 showing customer and prospect response rates by month.

Exhibit 6.7: Customer vs. Prospect Seasonality

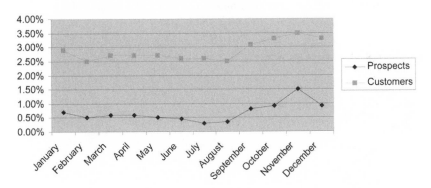

While prospects and customers seem to follow similar curves, the percentage variation is much greater for prospects. Customers vary from about 2.5 percent to 3.5 percent, while prospects vary from below 0.5 percent to 1.5 percent, with the highest season being more than three times better than the lowest. In addition, customer response rates warrant year-round marketing, while prospect response rates dictate seasonal marketing.

- How often do customers buy? The more often customers buy, the more appropriate it is to contact them frequently. The less often they buy, the less appropriate it is to contact them frequently.

Rather than use a chart or graph, think of this as simple human communication. Imagine a man asking a woman on a date. They go to dinner and have a nice time. The man calls her again and asks for another date. If she says she is busy, should he call her every day until she says yes? I think not.

Now imagine she says yes to the second date and that they begin to date regularly and see each other several times a week. Now, if the man calls every day, for one reason or another, is that not OK?

Dating examples aside, Exhibit 6.8 depicts a typical chart of the number of contacts per year for basic customer segments.

Exhibit 6.8: Contacts per Year

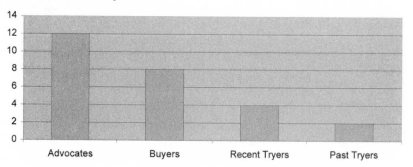

As you can see, advocates (the 20 percent of customers that make up 80 percent of sales) receive the most frequent communication, buyers receive less than advocates, new or recent tryers receive less than either advocates and buyers, and past tryers (small customers who haven't bought for a while) receive the least communication of all segments.

- How soon do they buy again after a purchase? For most consumable goods and services, customers are more likely to return sooner rather than later. A quick follow-up offer is generally most effective. Consider Exhibit 6.9, showing response rates from two different companies with customers segmented by recency.

Exhibit 6.9: Response Rate by Number of Months Since Last Purchase

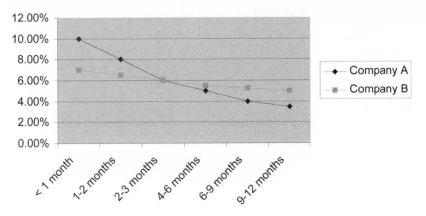

As you can see, customers from Company A are more likely to buy if contacted shortly after a purchase and much less likely if contacted long afterward. Company B has some decline, but much less. It is far more urgent for Company A to stay in frequent contact with their recent customers, while company B needs fewer communications immediately after a sale.

Where Do Best Customers Come From?

Many marketers seem to believe that new best customers come from outside the house file. However, this is usually not the case. In fact, new best customers move up within the house file. To devise a strategy to most effectively increase best customers, you need to answer the following:

- Are best customers moving up in the database or coming from the outside?

  A business-to-business seller analyzed his list and determined that of his customers who became advocates in the past year, nearly 90 percent had been tryers or buyers. Upon additional review of the 10 percent of advocates who appeared to be new customers, most turned out to be companies that had changed names or were acquired by other companies that were already customers. The business-to-business seller literally could count the new customers who became advocates on one hand.

- Is enough emphasis placed on keeping customers? Are current customers being ignored while the organization chases new prospects?

  A symphony was trying to increase overall subscriptions by prospecting heavily. Upon reviewing their data, they found their retention rate was down to 60 percent. By comparing their retention rate to those of comparable symphonic organizations, they learned that most rates were closer to 80 percent. By shifting the marketing focus to retention, they found they needed fewer new subscribers to grow.

- What is the right balance of marketing efforts between prospecting and retention?

  It is important to remember that retention drives prospecting, and not the other way around. Retention increases lifetime value, which increases the value and potential of prospects. Retention is the horse, prospecting is the cart.

  For example, a medical equipment manufacturer was looking for new dealers to grow their base of customers. They felt they had about 50 percent of the market, so they thought there were still a large number of dealers left to whom they could sell. To their surprise, they found that nearly every medical equipment dealer was buying at least some of their products. They didn't have 50 percent of the market; they did 50 percent of their business with almost 100 percent of the market. They learned from their data that they needed to focus on reassessing their account penetration strategy, not their market penetration strategy.

The company learned that they could not grow their business by finding new customers because there were practically no new customers left to be found. Instead, they had to grow their business by selling more to the customers they already had.

Which Media Are Most Effective in Making Contacts?

Marketers often select a favorite medium to reach buyers and prospects and tend to rebel when that medium is deemed ineffective for certain offers. For example, a marketer sending out 500,000 direct mail prospecting pieces is usually disappointed if they find out that only 250,000 are likely to be profitable, and that the mailing size should be reduced.

Rather than testing another media such as print, email, or broadcast, they may struggle to avoid reducing the use of their favorite medium. However, especially with the Internet, there is almost certainly a "media mix" that is appropriate for even classic direct marketers. To pursue that mix, some of the questions to answer include:

- Does a combination of media produce better results?

  For example, will a letter and an email out-perform a letter alone? Consider the chart in Exhibit 6.10, which is based on a retailer sending out flyers only, flyers and emails, and emails only to customers.

  As you can see, a combination of mail and email seemed to perform the best. Here is a note to the wise

Exhibit 6.10: Flyer and Email Response Rates

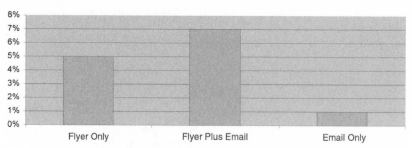

about segmenting customers and media when using opt-in emails: Generally, customers who will give you their email address will respond better than those who will not provide their email address. If this same company were to test mail alone for customers with email and mail alone for customers without email, they might find that customers with email respond better. Be sure you test not only the media, but the segments as well.

- Do some customers prefer one medium over another?

    For example, can some customers be eliminated from certain mailings and given emails instead, without a resulting loss in sales? Test this based on opt-in or opt-out selection, as well as on the media to which the customers best respond. Many organizations find they can reduce mail expenses by 20 percent or more by simply allowing customers who prefer an email to choose that option. Be sure to test, however, to see if the response rate of the email-only customers drops.

- Do general media, like magazines or radio, produce good prospects or information requests?

    Many organizations are afraid to use methods not traditional to their marketing methods to attract new customers For example, a cataloger that acquired most new customers through the mail tried direct-response cable TV ads. They found new customers from their TV ads were just as valuable as catalog buyers as were other new customers. Direct-TV gave them a whole new medium to use for finding new customers and growing their house file.

Many direct-mail catalogers now get most of their new prospects from their websites. Public relations (PR) communications that mention a website address are becoming a common way for companies to get new prospects, as people go to their website for more information. Tracking which media prospects come from, respond to, and prefer is critical in understanding what media are most productive.

House File Inventory

A *house file inventory* is the basic building block in developing a communication strategy for existing customers and prospects. A house file inventory describes:

- What segments are in the database
- How many contacts are in each segment

Without a house file inventory, organizations have to develop strategy without knowing how many segments they have or how many customers and prospects are in each segment. Unfortunately, this is quite common.

In its most basic form, any house file inventory has four segments. They are:

1. Advocates (the 20 percent that make up 80 percent of the business)
2. Buyers (make a few or occasional purchases)

3. Tryers (made one purchase or only sample purchases)

4. Prospects (not a customer, but a likely target)

Suspects are not part of a house file inventory, as they are not in the database.

Each of these four groups can be broken down further by:

1. How much they have spent in total

2. How much they spend on average

3. How many purchases they have made

4. How long ago they last responded or purchased

A most basic house file inventory might look like the following:

- Advocates   2,000
- Buyers   3,000
- Tryers   5,000
- Prospects   1,000
- Total Names: 11,000

While it may seem obvious that these basic segments should be contacted in different ways, with different degrees or frequency, many organizations do not do so. They may simply send out a renewal form to all current customers or contact everyone four times a year. Buyers who spend a significant sum of money may be treated the same as buyers who spend little.

Without a house file inventory, a marketer would likely treat all 11,000 people the same. With a house file inventory, describing and showing the quantities available in each segment, the marketer has a useful planning and management tool.

Effective analysis of customer and prospect behavior results in a better house file inventory. The house file inventory is the most crucial component in developing, tracking, and managing a communication strategy. Without it, successful data-driven strategy cannot proceed.

Quantifying the House File Inventory

Building your house file inventory demands some understanding of what makes segments different; managing your house file inventory demands understanding of what drives lifetime value or long-term profitability in those segments. While in-depth techniques to quantify and predict value and behavior will be discussed later in this book, the following questions highlight the main focus points involving customer behavior.

- About New Customers:
    1) How much does it cost to acquire a new customer?
        a. How much was spent advertising to reach prospects?
        b. How many new customers were acquired?
    2) How much are new customers worth in the first year, second year, and so on?
        a. How much will they spend in year one, year two, and year three?
        b. How much will be spent re-contacting them, selling, and supporting them?
    3) How much can you afford to invest in acquiring new customers?
        a. Are the profits generated from new customers greater than the costs to acquire them?
        b. How long can you wait for your return? Is a year too long?

Most organizations don't know the long-term or "lifetime value" of a new customer. As a result, they can only guess at how much they can afford to spend on prospecting. Some, like some of the now defunct dot-coms, spent too much. Other organizations look at overall customer value, but don't separate new from ongoing customers. They can't tell if they are growing because of new customers, or being carried by a few loyal customers.

- About People and Organizations:
  1) Who are the best contacts?
     a. Who actually makes the decision to purchase?
     b. Are the buyers, users, and decision-makers the same or different people?
  2) Which are the best locations?
     a. Do some locations buy for others, while some buy only for themselves, and others don't buy at all?
     b. Does size matter? Are big locations the best?
  3) Which are the best multi-location or multi-contact customers?
     a. Is the best customer really a corporation that is buying from many locations?
     b. Are the best customers the ones where buyers, users, and decision-makers are together and all included in the database?

Most marketers in business-to-business track customers one way—at the contact level, location level, or corporate level. Doing so only one way leaves many questions unanswered. For example:

- Are there non-buying influencers at locations with big buyers? A marketer tracking at the contact level would view them as non-customers.
- Is a corporate customer buying from many locations? A marketer tracking at the location level would see only several small customers, not one big one. A marketer tracking at the corporate level may be ignoring key contacts at specific locations.

- About Products:
  1) Which products are most profitable?
     a. Do some products have higher margins than others?

> b. Are some products easier to sell and require less marketing than others?
>
> 2) What products do the best customers buy?
>
> a. What items do the largest customers buy?
>
> b. Do some products need to be used together, like nuts and bolts or flashlights and batteries?
>
> 3) Do best customers buy many products or only certain products?
>
> a. Is buying the "full line" the mark of a good, loyal customer?
>
> b. Are products serving different markets, so that "best customer" segments appear with different products?

Many marketers carry assumptions about product-by-product profitability that are incorrect. Few marketing data systems carry accurate cost data at the item level, margins are often a guess, and product managers are usually unconcerned or unaware of multi-product buying patterns. For example, an organization selling a loss-leader product to retain its best customers found they seldom bought the low-margin item. An organization whose product managers each wanted a separate catalog found crossover buying exceeded 80 percent, and loyal customers always bought multiple products.

- About transactions:
  1) What is the average order amount?
     a. Does average order vary greatly by season or market?
     b. Do the offers tend to match the average order or are they inadvertently geared to creating much smaller orders?
  2) What is the median (typical) order amount? Is it near the average order?
     a. How many orders are below the "average"?

(Bearing in mind a few large orders can offset many small ones.)

   b. Are the typical and average orders what you would expect, given the offers, products, and so on?
3) How many of transactions are so small they are done at a loss?
   a. What does it cost to take (fulfill) an order?
   b. What is the smallest order that carries a profit margin high enough to cover fulfillment cost?

Marketers often ignore transaction costs and assume an average order is a typical order. For example, an organization with a $500 average order found 80 percent of its orders were $50 or less. A few very large orders inflated the average. Given their costs of taking and shipping an order, this represented a loss of about $20 for a typical order.

- About the 80/20 rule:
    1) How many of best customers comprise 80 percent to 90 percent of sales?
       a. How many or how few customers create the bulk of sales?
       b. Do they buy more or do they just buy more often?
    2) What characteristics are common in best customers?
       a. Based on demographics or firmagraphics, do they look different?
       b. Do they have similar buying patterns?
    3) Is the organization gaining or losing best customers?
       a. How many best customers have been acquired in the last year or two?
       b. How many best customers, based on data from a year ago, are no longer best customers?

Most marketers are shocked to learn how few customers really keep them afloat. In one extreme case, despite years of general advertising market-wide, a farm chemical manufacturer found that only six farmers comprised over 90 percent of sales for a particular niche chemical. Best customers, not the average customer, are the ones organizations should seek more of.

- About prospects:
    1) Do prospects look like best customers?
        a. Do they have similar demographics or firmagraphics?
        b. If they "look" different, are they in a potentially growing market, or are they just low-value targets?
    2) How many prospects exist that look like best customers?
        a. Can you define best customers and then identify similar prospects based on that definition?
        b. What percentage of the market are best customers based on that definition? What percent are remaining prospects?
    3) How valuable is prospecting compared to retention?
        a. Are repeat sales too low to justify acquisition cost?
        b. Is money better spent raising the value of existing customers, or attracting new customers at the same value as before?

Many organizations have lists of prospects that look nothing like their best customers. For example, one organization selling components to manufacturers had a $1,000+ average order, and their prospect list contained end-users who had an average order below $50. Another organization selling to pharmacists sought out a list of fresh names, only to find they already sold to well over 90 percent of the market. Commonly, marketers that emphasize prospecting learn that if they did a better job of retention they could afford to spend a lot more to gain new customers.

Building Budgets and Sales Projections Using the House File Inventory

Most sales projections are built top-down, in that they are based on last year's overall sales, and then revised (usually upward) by some percentage.

Using the house file inventory, communication budgets and sales projections can be built bottom-up. In other words, the communication plan can be laid out by segment with the expected costs and sales results.

For example, consider an alumni association with 10,000 members. They may seek a goal of 10 percent more members next year. As long as they either have been trending up in the past, or are planning to spend more to attract members, this may seem a reasonable goal.

Now, let's look at it from a house file inventory standpoint. First, let's look at the segments they are likely to have:

Segment	Members
Life Members	2,500
Repeat Annual Members	6,000
New Annual Members	1,500

With a goal of 10 percent more members, some may conclude that getting 1,000 alumni to join will meet the goal. But that is not the case. We need to consider renewal rates by segment as well:

Segment	Members	Renewal Rate	Renewals
Life Members	2,500	98%	2,450
Repeat Annual Members	6,000	75%	4,500
New Annual Members	1,500	50%	750

With the current renewal rates, the association will have 7,700 renewals. (Life Members don't live forever, that's why the renewal rate is 98 percent.) If the association attracts 1,500 new members, their membership will drop by 800. They need to attract 2,300 new members just to stay even, and 3,300 to achieve their goal.

Now the goal of a 10 percent increase becomes a goal of increasing new members by 220 percent.

Let's say they intend to first focus on retention and then go after a more reasonable increase in new members. While they cannot make life members immortal, they can reduce attrition through better communication with annual members. Consider the revised renewal goals:

Segment	Members	Renewal Rate	Renewals
Life Members	2,500	98%	2,450
Repeat Annual Members	6,000	85%	5,100
New Annual Members	1,500	65%	975

By focusing on retention, they can at least retain enough members to stay even at their current rate of acquiring new members. They will still have to attract 2,500 new members to reach a goal of 11,000 total. However, looking at very basic numbers such as these in a very simple house file inventory provides a much more useful and realistic set of information than overall numbers.

Creating a house file inventory and using it to build bottom-up sales projections and communication budgets both simplifies and focuses strategy.

The Process of Building a Business Model

Business modeling is most successful when driven by a team of knowledgeable individuals who are willing and able to extend expertise and understanding across corporate boundaries. Starting with a shared common goal, team members bring together different viewpoints, plus unique needs and abilities, that are crucial to the process of developing the business model.

Building a Team

Ideally, your team should be composed of people trained in many different disciplines and who represent all the major functional areas of your organization. From the outset, this team must be supported by top management, which in turn demands the added support of the leaders in each functional area. This means that staff in each area must be reminded to look at the larger picture and remain open to what's required of each area to make the business model better, rather than looking only at what is best for their particular area.

Often, it is assumed that a single area, typically IT or marketing, can take on a strategic leadership and management role and decide courses of actions for the business model by itself. In other cases a software vendor represents their system as a complete solution. Unfortunately, in most cases these types of approaches often produce poor results because they limit the knowledge base as well as the broad-based buy-in required for a successful retooling of the company's business model.

The basic reasons to have team members from different functional areas are apparent when reviewing the breadth and scope of knowledge and duties that each brings to the group. Particularly crucial is developing a team that includes both customer facing and company facing members. Some of the common examples are shared below.

- Sales persons provide firsthand understanding of customers, knowledge regarding contact strategies with top customers, deliver the point-of-sale information, and gather responses firsthand.
- Marketing offers insight about the marketplace as a whole through market research and industry data, plus background on corporate communication.
- IT brings knowledge of how the company has already stored data within existing systems and describes both the unused and active system capacities available at present and in the future.
- Accounting and finance manages crucial cost data and information about financial capabilities that must be incorporated when establishing the most profitable customers, products, and markets.
- Human resources are counted on to help understand the availability and limitations of expertise both within and outside the company and the ability of current personnel to absorb change.
- Top management represents internal company needs and

capabilities, coupled with investor expectations, market directions, and strategic needs.

The duties and expectations for each team member change as the development of the business model moves forward. For example, it is typical for organizations to document the cost of items sold in the accounting system differently from the way they are reflected in the order entry sales system. Accounting may aggregate costs by month, by supplier, or by plant, while sales may prefer to track cost by sale. It is unusual for someone in order entry to be required or to see any need to keep cost data accurate on an item-by-item basis, when costs are not tracked or managed using the order entry system. Most commonly, cost-of-goods becomes an agreed-upon percentage. As a result, costs when shown by item are often inaccurate on an individual item basis.

These types of inaccuracies may well cause a new and separate project to determine costs as accurately as possible on a transaction level for each item sold, and not just a periodic (monthly) level. These new data become a key input to new calculations and thinking as the analysis unfolds. It is but one example of the types of changes that can and will occur with a cross-functional team approach.

You can expect the work level for individual team members to ebb and flow while the initial database effort is being developed. During the initial phases new information is being requested that individuals have never had to communicate before or may not have been responsible for tracking. Top management should watch over the group to keep their operating friction to a minimum, by offering a system of rewards and measurements that encourages individuals to support the needs of the group. Otherwise, many of the required tasks and data inputs will be put on back burners to languish in obscurity.

Top Management as Director

The impetus to make certain changes initially can be detected anywhere in the organization. It remains up to top managers to direct strategy.

Major changes in the way a company does business, measures its own success, or describes the way it goes to market almost always require a push from top management to succeed. Anyone can feel the effects of operating friction, but only top management can exert enough push to overcome it.

Important strategic changes are rarely accomplished within only one department or functional area, and require the cooperation of people throughout an organization. Educating those both inside and outside the organization who will be affected by change is crucial to obtaining the necessary buy-in. It is one thing to say, "I want to do something you may disagree with." It is another to say, "I want to do something you may disagree with and here is why. . . ."

Top management has a unique ability, and that is to inject discomfort. The most satisfied people in an organization are often the least likely to want any kind of change. If someone they perceive as a peer or a subordinate attempts to change their situation, they will likely respond negatively. If top management wants too much to avoid angering anyone, they have lost a vital tool in being able to change the organization. Much like a angry parent rousing a late-sleeping teenager out of bed on a school morning, in order to drive meaningful change, top management must, at times, make the situation uncomfortable enough that it gets some people to move.

Avoiding the important task of explaining and selling the need for change and simply leaving any dirty work to others is not likely to produce positive change. It is likely to breed an undercurrent of resistance that will be hard to control and can potentially undermine the process. Relying on position, authority, or reputation is not enough. Expect to make your case several times, in several places. You may not find agreement on each point, but you can expand upon the points where you do find agreement.

People have a natural resistance to change. Even when the fear of the known exceeds the fear of the unknown, people may prefer to thwart change rather than accept it. Managers need to push for changes they see as important and seek to understand the reasons employees and others may be resistant. Sometimes reasons are obvious, such as fear of losing their job. Other times, the reasons are hidden and personal, such as fear of taking on a leadership role, working with a different group of people, or even changing their self-image when what they do is no longer the same.

Changing rewards and measurements may well have to occur in advance of any major, desired changes. Ultimately, people do what they are rewarded to do and it is the duty of top management to see to it that goals for desired results and the measurements and rewards for desired results are in sync.

Investors

Right or wrong, managers often feel that investors would rather they stick to some original plan than demonstrate how they can adapt to changing circumstances. Fear of change tends to hinder relationships among top managers and investors.

Managers fear telling investors that a change in strategic outlook is occurring (or more often, has occurred) and investors fear learning their money is being used differently than they expected. Realistically, both managers and investors have to admit that change is inevitable and that the organizations that adapt the most efficiently over time will eventually become the most successful.

Recognizing that managing the business model is by nature an adaptive process helps people understand that monitoring how well the business model is managed is more productive than monitoring whether or not it changed.

For example, if an organization that was gearing sales efforts to small businesses with five or fewer employees finds that most of its business comes from companies with 50 or more employees, managers would naturally shift some focus to larger customers. An investor that understood the circumstance would likely make the same decision.

For investors, gathering the information to monitor the health of the business model is the challenge. For example, it is easy for an investor to monitor how many passengers an airline carried in the previous quarter. It is not so easy to figure out how many passengers were business travelers or vacationers.

For an investor, a basic business modeling question, such as how much emphasis should be placed on businesses and how much on consumers, is quite hard to answer. As a result, it would be difficult for an investor to support or refute the need for changes in things like frequent-flyer reward programs or business-class seating.

It is important to keep predictions separate from decisions. That is, if a prediction is based on a predictable business model and the model can be revised into something better, the old model shouldn't be kept just because someone said it would work. Especially for small- to medium-sized organizations, the imagined core audience or even the expected use of a product may end up quite different than expected.

Facilitators

Facilitators are those who assist in the process of business modeling and are often the key to long-term success. They are usually outsiders, objective in perspective, experienced in such matters, and successful in the past. Facilitators should be hired by and report directly to top management.

Bringing in a different point of view and not becoming a part of the day-to-day culture is important. An outside consultant shouldn't try to become a permanent part of the organization. Generally, an older professional with more experience functions well in this role and is respected by the business modeling team.

It is important to point out that bringing in a consultant, whether a consulting professional, a business professor consulting part-time, or a semi-retired executive (ideally with experience from a different company or companies) is something that should be planned on from the start of the process.

The facilitator will play an important role throughout the process and is crucial to its success. Resist the temptation to avoid hiring an outsider until after insiders have clearly failed and the situation is so out of hand that an outsider is required.

The ideal facilitator may be an individual or a team, but either way must fulfill certain crucial roles. He or she:

- Should be able to perform tasks that cannot be carried out by internal departments.
- Should have expertise in activities that are part of the business modeling change process, but that are not likely to be repeated on a day-to-day basis (and as such, are not skills worth developing internally).
- Must be a neutral party, not selling a particular product or service (such as CRM software) and not tied too heavily to any one department.

Top management must be aware that each manager reporting to them has their own hidden agenda. Each wants to look as good as possible, both as an individual and as the head of their department. If one department controls a facilitator, he or she will not serve the facilitation purpose properly. For example, if marketing wants their own CRM system outside of IT and hires a facilitator from the vendor they would like to purchase from, the facilitator has lost their neutral role with IT—and with top management.

Performing in-depth statistical analysis of the organization's marketplace is an example of something smaller organizations may choose to have performed by or through a facilitator. Day-to-day analytical support is often very different than that required for business modeling, which makes it difficult to build or retain the talent necessary to do it in house.

Internal Lead Roles

The silos of an organization that are considered profit centers generally desire growth, and as a result, tend to expect at least some degree of change—to a point. Unfortunately, the tactical goals of a given silo may not match the strategic goals of the organization as a whole.

For example, consider IBM and the PC. Prior to the development of the PC, their sales department successfully sold mainframe computers to large organizations through individual salespeople. They were the best in the world at selling mainframe computers. It was well worth the high cost of highly-trained, expert salespeople, paid on commission, who could visit clients on-site, make recommendations, close the sale.

Unfortunately, that method of selling wasn't appropriate for PCs. Each sale was too small to be worth a salesperson's time, and only the largest companies buying many PCs at once (usually tied to a mainframe) were worth pursuing, given the rewards and measurements based on the sales department's tactical goals.

Did IBM fail to dominate the PC market because they believed their sales organization, as it was structured, was the best way to sell them? Did the sales department, which was highly respected and very powerful within IBM, kill efforts to sell PCs directly or through retailers? It was a combination of both, and either way, much to the detriment of IBM as a whole, the company failed to create a business model that would allow them to sell PCs profitably.

Top management needs to consider how costs and profits are rewarded internally (note, rewarded, not allocated) to balance the basic strengths and weaknesses the organization may have in the marketplace. Many a company has failed because one department was so successful they could block change elsewhere. In IBM's case, top management was unwilling or unable to inject enough discomfort into the sales department to force them to change, even though they clearly saw a need to do so. Eventually, the marketplace did it for them.

Support Roles

Departments that provide support services tend to seek stability rather than change. Information technology departments specialize in supporting planned systems that meet clearly pre-defined needs and have specific reporting timetables. Human resources seeks a stable work environment for employees and likely focuses more on controlling healthcare costs, reducing employee turnover or, managing benefits than building the workforce the company will need in five years. Accounting follows established financial procedures and seeks to support managing to a norm, either within the company or within the industry.

While any of the support departments can be a great launching area for a leader with vision, most of the pressure put on them is likely to be re-active rather than pro-active toward change within the company.

For example, IT and accounting certainly handle data that can be used for strategic analysis. While these departments may be quite good at determining if a system takes too much time to support or if an area of the organization is losing money, they may be less effective at building a plan to do something about it.

Accounting and finance may have to track details they may not have needed before, detail specific costs that may have been rolled-up in the past, and deliver new information. If it is simply seen as extra work, without understanding the reason(s) it is necessary, changes are likely to get back-burner treatment.

Information technology is a particular treasure-trove of knowledge in the form of data, if it can be harnessed. Unfortunately, many IT professionals, while skilled at managing systems or analyzing internal system functions, are not trained in managing the knowledge of the system. Accounting systems may be supported by IT professionals with no practical accounting experience, marketing systems may be supported by people with no practical marketing experience, and so on. Much like a security guard standing in front of a bank vault may not be an expert in financial management, an IT professional may not be an expert in the area their systems support. That is why managers with cross-pollination experience in IT and in other areas are so valuable.

There is also a general divide among people who build systems and those who operate them, much like the difference among aircraft designers and pilots. As a result, operators may know how to get what they need, much the way a pilot can make the aircraft go where he wants. But operators often don't know what else they can and can't gather or why they would look for some other kinds of data, much like the way a pilot may not know how to re-design an airplane like an aircraft designer could. Experience with managing IT systems is very different from systems design, just as flying aircraft is different from designing them.

The mere fact that IT, accounting, or HR generate or control data for tactical purposes that are highly important in the strategic business modeling process does not mean any given individual in those areas can lead a strategic initiative. However, the right people, with the right backgrounds, can greatly enhance their departments' strategic support capability. Developing strategic skills may require a push from top management, as tactical specialists may not develop them on their own.

Employees' Personal and Professional Strengths

Growing employees who can make and manage change is crucial to the business modeling process, where change can be quite dramatic. It requires telling people why things are done the way they are and allowing them a cross-silo view. When different silos operate on different systems and have completely different goals, this can be a challenge.

Most people prefer order to disruption. Given the choice, they'd choose boredom with familiar tasks over uncertainty with new tasks, even if they say otherwise. Soothing the fear of change, educating the fearful so they understand why a change is needed, and rewarding positive change is crucial.

Many organizations confuse training with change. By training managers in the latest management technique they hope some unforeseen, but positive change will occur. What they often end up with is a bunch of people who spend so much time in classes and seminars they don't have the extra time to make changes in their real jobs. There are times when a new technique is beneficial to the organization as a whole. However, most times it is more likely that individuals simply need a broader background.

For example, an IT professional with no marketing experience or training may benefit from understanding marketing better. An accounting professional might be more valuable to the organization in the long run if he was transferred into production for a year or two. A marketing specialist might learn by working in finance for a while. Even if moving someone across departments is not practical, cross-training may be. This training will be especially useful if department goals are linked and greater cooperation becomes essential to success.

The business modeling team is intended to bring together people with different points of view and different backgrounds. It may be necessary to allow some time for individuals to learn about other areas of the organization. Top management needs to support cross-silo cooperation, and make sure rewards, measures, and goals foster cooperation.

Once you have your team in place and understand the challenges you can expect to confront, what steps does your team need to move forward in the process of changing your business model?

Business Model Situation Analysis

The initial purpose of the following business model situation analysis and review is to provide a cursory understanding of an existing business model. Prior to analyzing the business model, it is necessary to conduct an initial review.

Initial Review

The initial review begins before data systems are built and loaded and continues throughout the entire process.

You begin by collecting information that has human meaning and understanding before collecting data; otherwise it will be "just numbers." In the following discussion, the word "data" will refer to either behavioral data, such as customer and transaction data, or descriptive data about customers and prospects. This can include household demographic data about consumers or data about individual businesses. The word "information" will refer to knowledge about the company, such as business plans, marketing strategies, metadata (data about data), and so forth.

The business model situation analysis will ensure that the database effort supports the needs of the enterprise. The process begins by using existing information to develop a basic understanding the current business model(s) that describe the following:

- Current business plan
- Current marketing strategy and tactics (subset of business plan)
- Current data structures, formats, expected data quality, and internal data availability
- The historical period covered by internally available data
- How revenue is reported, how costs are applied, and what reporting periods are used
- The annual revenue, approximate number of customers, and approximate number of transactions
- Outside marketing threats and opportunities
- Availability of secondary information outside the company
- Economic situation background (both external and internal)
- Comparison of current organization's structure to the organization's business plan and business model

Let's use an example of a small manufacturing firm that sells beauty products to consumers direct via catalog and the Web and to retailers who re-sell their products. We'll continue this example throughout the chapter. Here is what we might know about this company from the initial review:

- The company has been growing rapidly, over 45 percent per year and pursues new "retail" (direct) and wholesale customers aggressively through PR, magazines, trade shows, and direct mail. They have no outside sales force, produce all their own products, have very high quality, and costs that they believe are in line with their high quality. The company has been in business about eight years.

- Data are stored in either QuickBooks Pro (an accounting package) or Mail Order Manager (M.O.M.). All sales for the last two years (wholesale and direct) were recorded in M.O.M.; prior to that, all were recorded in QuickBooks. QuickBooks data go back three more years, for a total of five years of data that are available.

- Annual sales are $5 million a year, split among direct and wholesale. They had about 15,000 consumer customers last year and about 2,000 businesses. In addition, about 15,000 people per year request a catalog, mostly due to advertising or successful PR.

- They sell a premium product at a premium price to a crowded market, but other manufacturers in similar niches have done very well recently. Market size does not appear to be a limiting factor yet.

- Secondary information is readily available should they choose to obtain it for the consumers and retailers they typically sell to. They may be in a unique niche, but they do not perceive their customers are so unusual as to make gathering information difficult.

- The organization has chosen growth over profits and has relied upon investors to fund growth. Investors are willing to invest more, if the company can show it will make a profit.

- The organization is small and lean, and will need to hire if growth continues. Most of the management has been with the company several years and are used to wearing several hats. As such, they will use a facilitator to help with key business modeling issues.

Keep in mind throughout the process that the purpose of the team effort is to turn data into knowledge and then make these new insights into actionable decisions that bring improved results. At the start, the team must develop a thorough understanding of what a company does (or thinks it does), plus a knowledge of the types of data that are available before attempting to create a data system that will improve the usability of that knowledge.

Step One: Employ Database Marketing Methodology

The discipline of database marketing will be used to gather, load, check, clean, define, and report on data gathered in the business modeling process. Far less glamorous and much more labor intense than some of the advance analytical techniques that will be used later, this phase is nonetheless crucial to the success of the process.

This phase often requires a number of iterations before arriving at a usable and useful database. In most companies this is unavoidable for three main reasons:

1. Builders vs. Managers. In general, the people who build IT systems are not the people who manage IT systems. In addition, normal employee turnover typically means the current managers are often two or three generations of employees removed from the time when the system was

built. This can pose a challenge in defining and understanding the available data.

The difference between system designers and system administrators is like the difference between aircraft designers and pilots. Even the best pilots may not know why a wing was designed the way it was or what electronic features may be added in the future. Some questions that are asked will fall into areas the current system managers simply never needed to know or even think about. In such cases, extra time may be required to find the answers.

2. Area of Responsibility. People usually focus on performing tasks they are responsible for completing, which is strongly affected and reinforced by the measurements and rewards they receive. For example, IT normally focuses on system issues, while order entry is responsible for keying in individual sales.

If order entry does not enter contact names or enters things like "Attention Accounts Payable" instead of a person's name, that information will be stored and managed by IT. If marketing asks IT for a list of contacts, they will not receive a good list, but this will not be the fault of IT. Getting contacts' names into the system could very likely not have been a part of any one department's responsibilities nor part of their measurements and rewards structure.

As a consequence of these types of disconnects in legacy (existing) system inputs, some of the data requests will have incomplete or incorrect data. Time should be allowed to determine whether or not to correct the data when it is deemed crucial. If it is deemed important, then there remain the questions of how to secure the data, what it will cost, and ultimately whether it's worth the total resource expenditures to secure it in a usable form.

3. Requirements of Documentation. Data dictionaries,

operating manuals, and metadata in general tend to be operations focused. Documentation tends to be maintained
by IT, which has distinctly different knowledge requirements than other departments.

Knowledge about the data, such as why they were captured, what they are used for, how they were derived, and
who is responsible for entering the data are typically not a
part of documentation requirements. However, answers to
these questions are crucial to understanding why the data
exist in its current form.

Some of the documentation will need further explanation. It's a simple
fact that in most cases no one person can answer all the questions, as
they will cross over different areas of expertise.

Prior to building a database, it is necessary to define the expected
data components and make specific requests for internal and external
data. There should be a proposed data dictionary and a specific data request to fit the dictionary.

It is important to make it clear to each party furnishing data which
specific pieces of information they are to provide. Specific requests are
based on information uncovered in the situation analysis and business
model and include:

- Which individuals/departments will provide data
- Which files, fields, and records
- Expected documentation to accompany each file provided
- Expected deadlines

Even though the form of the database is likely to mutate as knowledge
is uncovered, it is still crucial to start from a well-defined point. Simply
"sending a copy of the data" is rarely an efficient beginning to a well-
planned project.

For our example company, the beauty products manufacturer, based
on Step One we now know several things:

- Nobody within the organization built their systems; all were "bought" systems created by outsiders. Company staff have enough skill to use their systems, but rely on outsiders for changes, upgrades, and so on.
- Every manager, at peak times and at others time throughout the year, works in order entry. As a result, information capture appears pretty good. However, there is some overlap of information from QuickBooks to M.O.M. and it is not yet clear which system contains more accurate and complete information on an individual sale basis.
- Outsiders created documentation about metadata. The business modeling team will have to start with what is available from the vendors of the two systems to understand data layouts and so on.

Step Two: Load Data

Loading the data is often much more than just entering the incoming data into a standard format so that the data can be manipulated and converted to match the data dictionary. Data received are often different than the data requested. It may be in an unreadable format or in a media format that is incompatible with the intended system.

Simply getting the right data to load can sometimes be a challenge. It may turn out that the request cannot be fulfilled as there is a misunderstanding about what data were available. It can take several attempts to get large systems to "talk to each other" when they use different input/output media. Often, the planned data structure changes as surprises are encountered when receiving data at the beginning of the project.

The reason for gathering the data is to have all business modeling data in a single database where analysts can begin the process of data assembly. Often, these steps are repeated, as data seldom arrive in a complete, correct manner on the initial attempt(s). This part of the process includes:

- Comparing data documentation to data requested for proper cataloging
- Physically loading data
- Converting data as necessary to a standard, usable database format
- Comparing data received to data requested
- Checking for completeness of data provided by field and record
- Re-submitting requests to replace incomplete or unusable data

Expect to encounter some difficulties in loading the data. Remember that until you have made the effort to fulfill a data request you may not know for sure whether that specific request can be fulfilled. Be prepared to change data requests and the proposed data dictionary as a result.

Loading data was a small challenge for our beauty products manufacturer. Information from the accounting package had to be downloaded through Excel spreadsheets, and then recombined. Special care had to be taken to make sure the same data were not included twice. The M.O.M. package, while easy to gather data from, had many pieces of data not needed for the process, such as what box something should be shipped in, which bin location an item could be found in, and so on. Extra time was taken with the data dictionary to fully understand what should be used, discarded, or reformatted.

Step Three: Data Check

The *data check* is the first opportunity to make sure complete, accurate data were received. It is based on a more in-depth review than a simple check of the layout of records and fields. Since many assumptions are made about the data before they are received, in cases where the data are known to be reliable based on reports that are already accepted, a data check will verify the data were received correctly and completely. In other cases, the quality of the data is unknown. The data check will indicate if the data are reliable or not.

The data check will uncover if data are incomplete, incorrect, or misinterpreted by the analysts before major expenses are incurred building the database. For example, sales amount may be off by a decimal point or sales from a given time period may be omitted. Resolving these discrepancies prior to the initial efforts to build the database will prevent major disappointments.

The data check should cover all data requested, but at a minimum, the following should be included:

- Number of invoices/transactions covering summary and product detail
- Sales dollars in total, by year, and by period
- Number of customers in total, by region, with purchases and without purchases
- Number of records with blank data in fields that can be expected to be populated
- Number of sales reps, products, and offers in the data provided
- Verification that key tables do relate to each other as expected by key fields such as customer number, invoice/ transaction number, product ID/SKU, and sales rep

Should inaccuracies be discovered in the data check, new data requests, and in some cases a revised data dictionary, will be required.

Most problems encountered during the data check are a result of miscommunication. Take special care to ensure that members of cross-functional teams communicate and work together during the data check process.

Likelihood of success is increased when you establish an expectation up-front that there will be problems understanding the data and that some data will be incomplete or incorrect. Rather than measuring success based on how good the data was when it arrived, you should measure team members based on how well they communicate their information and how well they respond to changes and requests for modifications.

For our beauty products manufacturer, a few small problems slowed down the data check. First, they had to review when sales were first recorded on a regular basis in M.O.M., and not QuickBooks. No one had kept track of the change date and several "test" entries, coupled with double entries during the change over, made that a challenge. Second, some of the fields did not mean what the team expected them to mean. For example, there were two customer IDs, but it quickly became apparent that one was a carryover from the old system and could be largely ignored. A field labeled "CustType" was thought to be the one identifying consumers vs. wholesale accounts, but it turned out to be a field labeled "CType." Once that was cleared up, the team proceeded to data hygiene.

Step Four: Data Hygiene

Data hygiene is virtually always needed to make the data clean, reliable, and of a consistent quality and format for analytical use in the database. This is especially true when data have been collected through different systems or entered by different groups of people.

It is important to uncover duplicate customer and/or prospect entries, make sure formats are consistent, and in some cases, create unique ID numbers. Steps needed to achieve thorough data hygiene include:

- Placing each data element in the correct field (often a problem with name/company/address data)
- Parsing names (for example, placing title/first/last name in separate fields)
- Parsing other data elements that may be incorrectly combined in one field

- Standardizing names, addresses, functional titles, and other categorical information as required, so that they are in a consistent format
- Finding, marking, and in some cases, eliminating duplicate records
- Creating unique ID numbers, as required
- Placing data into the data structures in the proposed data dictionary
- Creating exception reports for unusual findings and then *revising the proposed data dictionary and data request, if required*

Often *overlay data* (data from outside sources) are added to the database by matching contact records in the database. This should be done after cleaning the data and marking duplicates to ensure higher match rates and minimize the wasted expense of matching data to duplicate records.

Keep in mind that data from operational systems were never intended as inputs for business modeling; rather they were designed for the use in the system from which it came. Minor operational issues can become major issues for data standardization. For example, the company name "General Motors" could be simply GM. This won't cause a problem for those who are familiar with both titles, but could be a problem for someone trying to tie together hundreds of different company locations.

People use data differently and that can affect how the data are entered. For example, data coming from salespeoples' contact management software may contain very personal comments in a secondary address line such as "fat, but friendly," or "short guy with glasses." The salesperson may assume it is "their" data, so they enter whatever comments come to mind without realizing that the company will send mail to that person—comments and all. (True story) Beware of these kinds of problems and always consider the source when cleaning data.

For our beauty products manufacturer, data hygiene had some challenges. If only their products worked on data. First, they had not planned on having many wholesale accounts when they switched to M.O.M. As a result, there is no Company Name field, and company name winds up in either the Address One or Address Two lines. There is no room for information such as Title or Department. Second, they found catalog request names often re-entered when they made a purchase. This put several thousand duplicate names that they did not know they had into their system. Finally, they found they had gathered many names with no Source, and they did not know where these names came from. The result was that they dropped old names with no source.

Step Five: Set Data Dictionary

Once the hygiene portion of the project is complete, it is time to update the data dictionary, based on your experience with the available data. In addition to an accurate description of the tables, records, and fields in the new database, it now should be possible to describe the contents of coded fields so that the data become more useable.

The data dictionary should describe all fields, whether or not are they are always populated. For example, if sales information contains product numbers for the last 12 months only, that should be stated in the data dictionary. The updated information in the revised data dictionary should be much more complete than that in your proposed data dictionary.

Revisions to the data dictionary include:

- Revising field descriptions and file layouts
- Revising tables and entity relationships as needed
- Planning future update information requests and procedures to match the most current needs of the business modeling database

People will tend to have enough information about their data for them to do their jobs, but not more. It will require some time and effort to document the data in such a way that others can use it efficiently. Expect to work through the data hygiene process before a data dictionary that will provide the documentation needed to support analysis can be built.

For our beauty products manufacturer, setting the data dictionary was relatively simple. Nearly all the inside data they would use going forward would come from M.O.M., so once they learned how to prepare that data, they were very close to having a work-in-progress data dictionary. The biggest changes were reformatting the name and company fields. They may choose later to add to the data dictionary as they add summarized data about consumers, survey data, demographic data, and so on, but first they will analyze what they have and then decide what changes are merited.

Step Six: Create Reports Describing the Data

Armed with clean data and a useful data dictionary, it is now possible to build reports that describe the relationships occurring in the data.

Although basic, the descriptive reports created at this phase are more complex than those needed for the data check. For example, data check reports would look at how many sales dollars can be accounted for in the data provided to determine if the right data were sent and if the data were interpreted properly. A descriptive report would consider how much was spent by each customer and rank customers by total spending.

The reason for these more detailed reports is to provide a general understanding of buying patterns in the database. Such reports typically include:

- All reports from Step Four (data hygiene) based on clean, de-duplicated data in the final data structure
- Customer summary reports showing number of buyers by sales dollars, frequency of transactions, dates of transactions, and customer type (type/size of business, etc.)
- Define "best" customers (80/20 rule)
- Show sales by past marketing efforts, if possible based on data available

- Calculate and summarize life-to-date sales by customer,
  customer type, and marketing source

A distinction among reports created earlier for the data check and for
those created at this step to describe the data is that the latter will improve knowledge and understanding, while the former simply confirms
what is already known.

Another distinction between the reports is that data check reports
report one variable at a time. For example, are sales dollars accurate?
Do we have the right number of customers? Reports describing the
data tend to be cross-tabulation reports, showing the relationship of
two variables such as sales vs. customers, sales vs. product type, and
so on.

For our beauty products manufacturer, the cross-tab reports reveal
some basic, simple truths. First, even though they have an average
order around $65, most buyers tend to spend less. (See Exhibit 7.1.)
This is typical, as a few large orders tend to skew the average.

Exhibit 7.1: Number of Buyers by Average Order

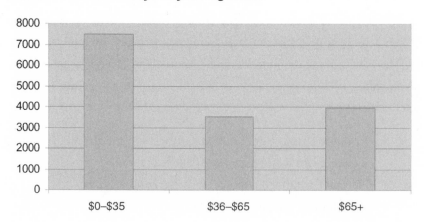

Initially, they found most of their buyers were one-time buyers and
that they had fewer repeat customers than they expected.

Exhibit 7.2: Number of Buyers by Frequency

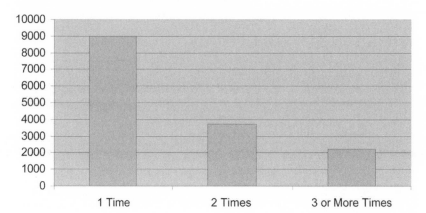

As we can see in Exhibit 7.2, most buyers bought once, some bought twice, and a few bought three or more times. This made it clear that they needed to get more repeat sales. Too few people became loyal buyers.

Next, they looked at how long ago buyers had last made a purchase. Clearly, they were growing their customer base, with nearly as many buyers in the last 90 days as they had in six months just over a year ago. (See Exhibit 7.3.)

Still, the chart also reveals a lot of inactive customers, many with no activity in over 24 months. Clearly, a large number of customers have simply churned through.

Exhibit 7.3: Number of Buyers by Recency

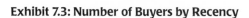
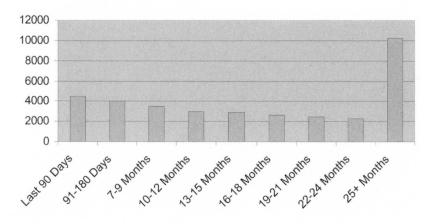

Exhibit 7.4: Response Rate by Recency of Request

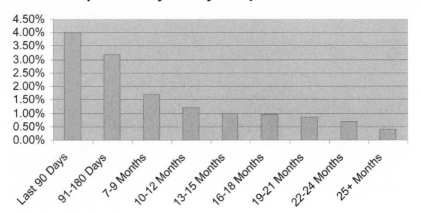

They found recency was in important factor in response for both customers and prospects. Simply looking at response rates from prospects to their catalog revealed they should focus more on recent prospects and less on older prospects. (See Exhibit 7.4.)

Clearly, money was well spent on quick follow-up, but contacts after a year were largely wasted.

Looking to find the 80/20 rule and to get an idea of who their best customers are, the manufacturer looked at one cross-tab that pointed to frequent buyers as being very valuable. (See Exhibit 7.5.)

Exhibit 7.5: Average Lifetime Spending by Frequency

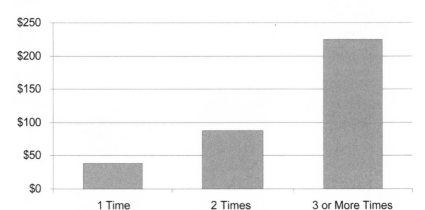

Lifetime spending of two-time buyers was well over twice that of one-time buyers (showing bigger buyers are more likely to repeat) and buyers making three or more purchases have lifetime values nearly six times higher than one-time buyers. This made them look more to repeat purchasers as a way to grow their business and not just to attracting new, one-time buyers.

Cross-tabulation reports do not describe complex, multivariate relationships, but they do tend to increase knowledge among managers familiar with the organization. Plan on having a summit meeting to review the knowledge uncovered. Actionable, useful changes to the business model are likely to occur as a result of the knowledge that has been secured up to this point in the project.

Step Seven: Data Mining

Data mining is a process that allows analysts and sophisticated managers to build knowledge by uncovering complex relationships within the data. These relationships may be apparent only across multiple data sets or through multiple variable relationships, or they may be simple relationships that can be clearly spotted through trends over time.

During the data check, variables were reviewed one at a time. The initial reports describing the data primarily compared one variable against another. For the some managers, this may appear to be sufficient. However, more complex relationships are certain to be occurring and should be understood before a final set of recurring reports is created.

Determining profitability is more complex than subtracting cost of goods sold from sales. There are discounts, rebates, marketing expenses, fixed costs, delivery costs, and other factors that play into profitability on an overall and a customer-by-customer basis. Data mining considers the interplay of these factors in describing what makes a customer profitable or likely to be profitable.

A simple example of this logic can be found using charts of height and weight. Assume we wanted to determine how healthy people are, based on how much they weigh, compared to an average sample of healthy people. First, we would check heights and weights separately. If a height was recorded that was too high or too low, say one person was 12 centimeters high and another was 2 kilometers tall, we would correct or eliminate that data.

We could then produce a cross-tabulation of heights and weights to identify how much people would be expected to weigh, given their height. For some, such a chart is quite sufficient in determining how much a person should weigh. However, many other factors play into how healthy a person is, besides height versus weight. Muscle mass, bone mass, lung capacity, age, gender, degree of exercise, and amount of calories consumed per day all factor into the equation. Data mining will help define this complex relationship and lead to a better understanding than simply comparing height and weight alone.

Despite considering multiple factors, data mining may even lead to a simpler way of making decisions. For example, percentage of body fat alone may be a sufficient means of determining if a person is over- or underweight, regardless of the other factors.

Many organizations try to skip the data mining phase or approach it as something that can be done by an analyst without a full understanding of the business model. Those that do so, do so at their peril. Without effective data mining, the systems that support business modeling and business decision-making in general, cannot reach their full potential. Rather than adding to the cost, data mining leverages the cost of the other data systems.

Data mining is typically approached as a technical challenge. Vendors would have you believe that if you get a big enough data warehouse, with fast enough computers, and load all the data you can get into it, voila! A successful data mining effort is born! If only it were that easy.

If the purpose of data mining were to build a big, impressive computer system that your vendors and IT department could be proud of and brag about to other techies, most data mining efforts would be a complete success. Unfortunately, most corporate data mines end up getting little or no use and are financial failures.

The purpose of data mining should be to build knowledge and understanding in order to make better decisions. The idea is that decisions based on hard, factual data are more reliable. Technical knowledge contributes to the availability of data, but not necessarily to the usefulness or understanding of the data.

Before you make any commitments to buying large computer systems to support data mining, be aware of this: Business modeling does not come in a box. It isn't a piece of software. There is no such thing as a computer system, CRM system, or data warehouse that will solve all your problems or answer all your questions. Data mining is a process, just as business modeling is a process and CRM is a process. New computer systems may, or may not, be required. Spending more does not equate to greater success (though it may), but it can certainly equate to greater failure. But either way, simply spending money on computers is no guarantee that the process will be a success.

Most data warehouses are full of space—and spaces. Literally, most data warehouses (which is where data mining is done) are over-designed in an attempt to capture everything about everybody. The business challenge of understanding the data is ignored by technical specialists, who instead focus on the technical challenge of storing data nobody understands.

The results are that the burdens of using data from a system designed to store lots of stuff, but not designed to support specific needs are so great that users quickly find reasons to avoid using the new system. The burdens of capturing and storing data that gets little use causes support people to quickly realize they have better things to do, so they will skip the work of loading in current, potentially useful data. So, the data warehouse spins happily away, storing spaces instead of data.

Data mining is best done in the same way that other mining is done.

- Know what you're looking for before you start.
- Do a high-altitude "fly by" to see if any territory looks like it might hold something interesting.
- Get the permission of the territory owner to do some preliminary exploration. (You'll not get far if you're trespassing someone's property in your search.)
- Extract some ore samples and test their quality to confirm that the ore is good enough to mine further. (You might be dealing with bad data.)
- Establish a consistent method and methodology to extract the data, so that each time you tap into the ore, you get consistent results. (Don't shoot down your conclusions with inconsistent data extraction procedures.)

The best data mining is done by end-user domain experts, specialists in different areas, like marketing, research, production, and so forth, not by the IT staff or the programmers. Too often, the IT staff does not understand the business relationships between the data elements—and this understanding is crucial to making sense of the data. Technical understanding is important, but no data mining effort can succeed without involving people with an understanding of the business and the businesses objectives.

Involving domain experts from across the business modeling team at an early stage is crucial to prevent corporate data systems from becoming clogged with too much data that are incorrect or incomplete.

For example, many systems used for sales support have a place for product cost. However, costs are managed by another department and tracked on another system. As a result, it may not be possible to track costs accurately by product with data in the sales support system. Determining this early on, before decisions are made based on bogus costs, is crucial.

Before undertaking a major data mining decision, ask two important questions:

1. What problems are we trying to solve?
2. Who understands the problems?

As you move ahead, stay focused on the problems, involve the people who understand them, and use technology as a means, not an end.

For our beauty products manufacturer, the purpose of data mining was to see if further analysis would support findings leading to growth. They knew they had a growing company, but they also discovered they had many prospect names to whom they were mailing that did not respond. They found that prospecting appeared to be more effective before the holiday season, but customers bought year-round. Customers making larger orders appeared more loyal over time. Based on these findings, they decided to proceed and find ways to simplify the complex relationships, so they could better understand their customers.

Step Eight: Exploring and Defining Relationships

Before going into an exploratory analysis, it is important to determine which behaviors are important to manage (such as revenue levels, loyalty, defection, profit, and product category sales) and what factors are related to those behaviors (such as number of past purchases, number of employees at a customer location, etc.).

From an analytical viewpoint, it is necessary to determine precisely what is being predicted (the dependent variables) and what is being used to predict (the independent variables). Results should include:

- Expectations for the process of statistical analysis and review
- Description of the relationships to be analyzed
- Definitions of what are to be predicted or described
- Definitions of dependent (predicted) and independent (predictor) variables

While it would appear that deciding what should be predicted or described and what should be used to predict or describe is simple logic, it often is misunderstood.

For example, determining what a person should weigh based on their height makes sense, as the assumption is they can control their weight. One could look at the weight of the author and determine he needs to increase his height by 20 centimeters, but there is little the author could do about that. However, the author could lose some weight if he were to try.

Make certain it is clear what the team is setting out to do at this stage, and keep communication open about discoveries while data mining. An open mind and a little teamwork here can save a lot of misunderstanding later.

For our beauty products manufacturer, they want to know what correlates to response (who will order and who won't), loyalty (who will continue to buy over time and who won't), and how much someone is likely to spend (average order per sale). They plan to take the information and use it to improve their strategy for contacting customers and prospects.

Step Nine: Create Descriptive Statistics

Creating descriptive statistics prior to modeling will show patterns within each variable and among each dependent (predicted) variable's relationship to each independent (predictor) variable.

Descriptive statistics can be created quickly for many variables using data mining and statistical analysis software. Statistics such as mean (arithmetic average), median (middle or mid-point value), mode (most common value), and standard deviation (an average of how much the data varies) can tell analysts a great deal about patterns in the data, as well as what to expect when using more advanced statistical techniques.

Examining basic statistical relationships that are occurring in the data assists in selecting the appropriate advanced modeling techniques. Results from creating descriptive statistics include:

- Cross-tabulated relationship reports for all pairs of important independent variables

- Confirmation of relationships or a lack of relationships among pairs of major variables
- Demonstration of which variable relationships are strongest and most likely to be predictive and/or descriptive

For most projects, creating descriptive statistics is straightforward and performed mainly by the analytical portion of the team. However, surprises do occur that may require the attention of the entire team. The most common surprise found at this stage is when two variables that were thought to be related turn out not to be.

For example, in the trucking industry, it was assumed that trucks carrying heavier loads would have larger engines than similar trucks carrying lighter cargo. The idea was that more bigger engines should be marketed to companies hauling heavier loads. In fact, even though it was expected, no such relationship was confirmed by the data. This discovery led to further discussion and research since it took a strong argument, supported with solid data, to prove to industry experts that one of their long-held basic assumptions was wrong.

Be prepared to look more deeply at relationships that are very different than conventional wisdom expects. It may take some time to review these surprises before the team as a whole accepts the information (factually and emotionally).

For our beauty products manufacturer, they made several discoveries from basic statistics. For example, they had thought women were better customers for them than men, since they had many more women than men buying from them. Instead, they found their male customers were just as good, on average, as their female customers.

	Average Order	Average Frequency	Average Lifetime Value
Women	$65.50	1.75	$114.63
Men	$66.12	1.73	$114.39

They also found that customers who bought several items were more loyal than those who bought only once. This correlated with their findings that people making larger average orders were more loyal as well (more items means a larger order).

Step Ten: Predictive and Descriptive Modeling

Predictive modeling should create statistical models to estimate revenue and loyalty for customers and potential customers. Descriptive modeling allows a "plain-English" means of communicating how customers are different.

Whether using a predictive or descriptive model, the results should be based on an analysis conducted by and also used by those who understand the business model. Different techniques offer different advantages and disadvantages. Knowing what you have and what you are trying to do with what you have is very important.

The reason for using predictive and descriptive modeling is to maximize understanding of the data prior to setting final reports. Discoveries from modeling typically have a major impact on which reports will be used for which purposes, what the contents will be, and how they will be used. Results include:

- Predictive modeling for selection/de-selection of customers and potential customers in future communication efforts
- Descriptive modeling for showing differences and similarities among customers and potential customers that help to create different messages or offers to different customers and prospects
- Recommendations on how to best use the knowledge discovered in the modeling process

Often modeling takes a different direction than expected. For example, in working with an alumni association (described in Chapter Two), we found no correlation among any combination of demographic variables and the likelihood of becoming a member. The only thing that correlated with becoming a member was involvement in any post-graduate university-related activity. Since only a small percentage of graduates had been active with the university and a low percentage overall were members, no useful predictive model could be built.

However, knowing that involvement led to membership, it was possible to create a descriptive model that put graduates into different lifestyle and life-stage segments. Armed with this information, it was possible to create activities that would appeal to alumni, thus increasing both involvement and membership.

In other cases, it may be found that no one or two things by themselves predict behavior. A predictive model can find the combination of variables that best explains response rates or average sale amounts. Since most people have a hard time explaining how a combination of six, eight, or ten things all work together, advanced modeling techniques can help explain things that people might otherwise be unable to easily explain. To get the most from predictive and descriptive modeling the analysts need to fully communicate their findings to the team. Best results are achieved by combining the expertise of the statistician with the entire team's knowledge of the business and understanding of the business model. It is very important for the entire team to consider as a group how the models will be used and what the findings of the modeling process mean before completing this phase.

For our beauty products manufacturer, they found recency (how long ago someone made an order or requested a catalog if they are a prospect), frequency (how many times they have ordered), and average orders were highly predictive and excellent segmentation tools. Demographics had little effect, as did lifestyles. They found their better wholesale customers tended to be smaller retailers, but whether or not they ordered many products or a few (if they sold the whole line the generally sold more) was more important than the size of the retailer. It should be noted they had no large retailers in their database.

Step Eleven: Create Final Report Set and Define Update Report Set

Defining and creating the final report based on the knowledge gained through the analysis completed to date, including the predictive and descriptive modeling, ensures the most useful and actionable reports possible. As team members use these they will gain new insights and develop more knowledge as the process moves forward.

As reports and content are defined, regular update procedures and requests must also be determined. Results from this phase include:

- Reports created to support and transfer knowledge gained throughout the business modeling process that should be periodically updated for future review and reevaluation. Has anything changed? Are there new insights?
- Procedures for future updates, including timing and data requests
- Development of an ongoing procedure to update and revise the database

Generally, people don't like reports, but they are necessary for transferring information. Efficiently compiling regular, periodic reports will support the on-going needs of the business modeling team. The team should consider which pieces of information are most crucial, what they plan to do with the information, and how they plan to track their progress when determining which reports they expect to use on a regular basis.

For our beauty products manufacturer, they decided to create reports tracking their customers' behavior from segment to segment on a monthly basis. This can be done more or less frequently, depending on the season and the various communication activities involving customers.

Step Twelve: Develop and Implement Strategy Based on Findings

The team should review their findings, discuss the implications, and set-up a strategy to implement their findings.

Make sure decision-makers understand the information available and give them a chance to revise their strategy decisions in marketing and other areas, based on the new knowledge. At this juncture in the process companies usually launch major new positioning and communications changes that are designed to take advantage of opportunities for improved results.

Results from developing (or revising) and implementing strategy include:

- Presentation(s) to others in the organization, with an explanation of the final report set for all intended users
- Review of implications for marketing, production, and sales
- Discussion of how to best use the data, changes to make immediately, and changes to make longer term

The first use of the knowledge gained through business modeling often results in such large changes that they must be phased in over time.

For example, a new sales group or department needs to be created for medium-sized accounts because they are too small for field sales reps to adequately manage. Or, it may require the phasing-out of certain product categories along with the phasing-in of products or services not offered in the past. These types of major changes result from insights gleaned from the process of developing the business model.

The result of even the best intentions to use the knowledge will result in surprises, the need for more research, and some degree of trial-and-error testing. Expect to create a plan that takes into consideration where the organization is, where it is going, and how it intends to get there.

For our beauty products manufacturer, they went with a simple strategy:

- More recent, more frequent customers were contacted more often.

- Prospects were contacted quickly, but only re-contacted a few times if they did not buy.
- The catalog and website were re-designed to increase average order and encourage larger orders (based on their findings that customers who spent more were more loyal) with offers often bundling several different products together.
- Research larger retailers, since none are in the data to track. That is left for future testing.
- Continue to create products that fit seasonal purchases (increasing frequency) and that encourage customers to buy multiple products.

Step Thirteen: Adjustment Period and Scheduled Updates

The adjustment period allows the organization to monitor how the database and the knowledge it provides are being used, receive feedback based on actual use, and make changes as required.

The reason for the adjustment period is to be able to react to the kinds of knowledge that can be derived only from using the database. It allows for a phase-in period prior to creating an automated reporting mechanism that will be difficult and expensive to change.

The adjustment period typically covers several reporting and update cycles so that users have time to see the results, react to them, monitor activity, and request needed changes. During the adjustment period, the database structure (as defined in the data dictionary) is kept as simple and flexible as possible to allow for changes.

Results from the adjustment period include:

- Completion of several update and reporting cycles
- Phase-in of more extensive use of the knowledge derived from the database
- Review of database usage and results
- Review of tracking capabilities of the database, to ensure results are being measured both accurately and completely

- Implementation of changes to the database and reports where practical and feasible

The use of an adjustment period for reviewing the database and making adjustments is very different from the process of buying or building a software application prior to implementing use of the data. The focus during the adjustment period is on knowledge, data, and useful information.

The processes of formalizing the computer screens, automating procedures, and investing in software development is put off for later. The intention is to make changes as cost-efficient as possible prior to a full-scale development project to build access tools for managers outside the business modeling team. The realistic assumption at this stage: It is simply impossible to know what is most important or useful before employing the data in live applications and decision-making where results are tracked.

Expect the adjustment period to last from several months to over a year. For seasonal businesses a decision to stay in the adjustment period through at least one major season can be smart, as it shows what happens when the system is at full capacity. The knowledge to support CRM should be available throughout the process, but changes should be allowed and expected.

For our beauty products manufacturer, a 12-month plan was put in place to use the findings. Twelve months was chosen for two reasons: (1) results had to be tracked across the seasons and (2) changes were large enough (with the catalog and website redesign) to require that much time to fully implement and track. Results were tracked, and data were fully re-analyzed at the end of the year. Results were encouraging, with sales up over 50 percent from the prior year.

Step Fourteen: Application Development

The purpose of application development is to create data access tools that automate much of the update process and transfer the right pieces of knowledge to the appropriate decision-makers in the most efficient manner possible. The importance of making sure the applications systems are user-friendly cannot be stressed too much.

The final system acts as both a decision-support system and an *enterprise resource planning system* (ERP), with the emphasis on supporting understanding at the business modeling level.

The results from application development include a:

- Proven set of requirements for final implementation
- Defined dataset and update procedure
- Useful set of reports and established data query needs
- Data access tool available for direct client use

The data access tool may reside anywhere on the Web, on a service provider's system, or on the client's network. With the data structure and outputs having proven their capabilities, software application developers can create a final product for the client with capabilities already proven effective.

It will be necessary to tailor the information needs based on the responsibilities of managers in different functional areas. Each department represented in the business modeling team will have different needs and different people will require different levels of access. In addition to the system supporting resource-planning needs throughout the organization, some planning must go into determining how the most precious of resources—information and knowledge—will be shared.

It is important that *all* steps prior to application development are completed *before* application development begins. Designing an interface and customizing access tools prior to being confident of the various data needs will result in disappointment with the final product and require expensive changes.

For our beauty products manufacturer, minor system changes were needed. They found orders from the Web did not usually have any key code, so they could not tell which offers their Web customers were responding to. They largely solved this by building a tracking mechanism into their data warehouse that matched mailed lists (with key codes) against sales that did not have a key code. They also discovered through the analysis at the end of the first year that many of their best customers sent their products as gifts, so they built a tracking mechanism to learn who the gift givers were and who the gift recipients were. They have yet to make a major investment in software and probably will not need to do so for another four or five years. Until then, the company continues to use their facilitator occasionally and still uses outside support for updating their more complex analyses.

Changing the Business Model

A data-based or fact-driven approach to management encounters is a natural obstacle that any organization may face when confronted with change. These natural obstacles are quite different than the technical issues that are usually seen as the challenge. Rarely are the real challenges purely technical.

An awareness of things that create a need for change is important. Whether the organization is running from a consequence, running toward a goal, or both, it helps you to define the strategy if you have an understanding of what is driving the pressure for change. (See Exhibit 8.1.)

The Pressure for Change

The real challenge of managing a business model is the deployment of people, knowledge, and skills. That done, deployment and use of technology will often follow. Particularly for those with a technical focus, awareness of the human and organizational issues that affect the way people interpret facts or data will make for more effective management of the business model.

Before making any fundamental change to the business model, it is important to consider winners and losers within the company. For example, a company selling exclusively through sales reps may determine that a large segment of current and potential customers are underserved, or cannot become profitable customers due to lower potential volume and the high selling costs of individual sales reps.

In such a case, the salespeople will almost certainly oppose the addition of a direct sales channel, such as telesales or a website. They may demand that a website be used for customer service and lead generation only, and not for sales. They might insist that they be entitled to full commissions on any sales made to customers in their territories, and so on.

An automobile manufacturer may be producing a sub-standard component, such as a fuel pump that is very noisy, and allowing dealers to solve the problem by replacing the defective fuel pumps with those from another manufacturer. The division producing the component may insist that they continue to make it until it can be re-designed, forcing the production of a known problem component for months or years. (True story)

One department, such as marketing pointing out the need to re-

Exhibit 8.1: Pressure for Change

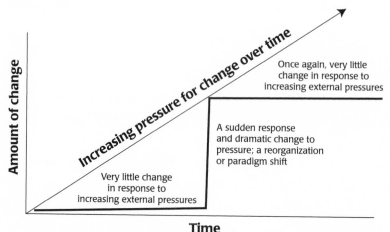

structure the sales department or the sales department pointing out the need to re-structure manufacturing, will result in little more than a squabble without top management taking the necessary leadership role.

The idea that top managers will be among friends while driving the necessary changes is unlikely to hold true. Often, the best decisions will be very difficult, both personally and professionally, for their more junior colleagues to accept.

Hysteresis

Hysteresis is the way many things, organizations, and people respond to change. While the term applies in the physical sciences, such as magnetism, metallurgy, electricity, and so on, it applies to people and organizations, too.

Specifically, hysteresis describes the way many things respond to change by being "sticky." That is, things stay the way they are until the pressure for change exceeds some threshold. The "straw that broke the camel's back" is a loose example of hysteresis. The camel didn't bend, like a rubber band, when loaded. Rather, it stood until that last straw was too much and then it changed dramatically.

For example, a light bulb will glow with the right amount of electricity. Too little and it is dark, too much and it burns out. A bridge might support one truck, or two trucks, but collapses under three trucks. It takes much more energy to boil heated water than it does to simply warm it a few degrees.

Organizations of many people tend to be more like brick walls or oak trees that resist change, rather than springs that adjust to change or willow trees that bend in the wind. Only when enough pressure is exerted to bring about change (any change) can a major change occur. Once that change is made, organizations are likely to stick to their new positions until another powerful force causes an additional change.

For example, General Motors realized that with their improved systems integration with their dealers, it was no longer necessary and quite expensive to have field sales and service reps calling on their smaller dealers. These smaller dealers tended to be in rural areas, far apart, and took a lot of time to physically visit on a regular basis.

They decided to build a centralized office where reps could call smaller dealers on a regular basis, rather than drive from one dealership to another. In order to do this, they had to relocate dozens of people and close several field offices. They could not make the change one dealership or one sales rep at a time.

Such a major change takes time to implement, and even more time to judge its effectiveness. As a result, the new contact strategy was in place several years before any major changes were attempted again. Fortunately for GM, this change was a success.

Adoption Hurdles

Adoption hurdles are specific points of change that must occur before any major change can go into effect. Successfully completing one adoption hurdle will not produce meaningful change; rather all the necessary adoption hurdles must be completed before a change can occur.

Adoption hurdles can mirror corporate silos and functional departments, and the hierarchy within each department can represent adoption hurdles. For example, a marketing director wants a CRM system. She will likely need approval or support from the IT director and will also need support from a CEO or COO.

The corporate hierarchy functions as a series of adoption hurdles. A mid-level engineer designs a component that must be approved by other engineers above him. Marketing and sales have to like it, distribution has to be able to handle it, and so on.

Comfort zone blindness is a serious adoption hurdle that can arise throughout the organization. People don't want to change when things are going well. Resistance to change will be high especially in the corporate silos that appear to be doing well. Many times, the longer a company or division has been successful, the longer they will tolerate being unsuccessful before they are willing to change.

Adoption hurdles are critical to the success or failure of any efforts to change the business model. It is important for top management to be aware of these hurdles and to step in when they need to help clear them.

Disruptive Technology

Disruptive technology is a new technology that offers different performance and different benefits than older, existing technologies. For manufacturers of steam locomotives, the diesel locomotive was a disruptive technology. For makers of large, powerful computers, smaller, but increasingly more powerful PCs and laptops are a disruptive technology. For makers of PCs and laptops, PDAs and advanced wireless phones are disruptive technologies.

It is important to be aware of disruptive technology, because traditional management and marketing methods will often overlook the opportunities and threats it may pose. Existing technologies generally appeal most to the mainstream, most profitable customers, i.e., the advocates. Disruptive technology may at first appeal mainly to less important customers, the tryers and a few buyers or to entirely new markets that may not even be prospects or suspects. This can give an organization a false sense of security while new technology matures if it does not at first appear to threaten their core markets and best customer advocate relationships.

For example, consider how wireless phones have changed the marketplace for local phone companies and for long-distance companies. Demand for land lines is going down and some people have only a wireless phone. They don't feel they need a phone wired into their homes anymore. Many people use wireless cell phones for long distance, so they don't need a traditional long-distance company.

Most of the largest wireless phone providers are either new companies, or separate companies set up by existing phone companies. Sprint

PCS was set up as a separate company from Sprint Long Distance and from Sprint's local services. Had Sprint management not had the foresight to make PCS separate, it is likely that internal squabbles would have prevented it from entering the marketplace.

The long-distance division of Sprint certainly didn't like to see long-distance minutes included with cell phone plans. The local division certainly didn't want to see people drop their land lines and have only a wireless phone. If PCS had started out as a part of the other divisions, it is doubtful that it could have competed in the marketplace.

Disruptive technology is usually brought to market by new organizations or divisions that operate with a different and often autonomous business model than the organizations offering mature technology. The price points, average sale, sales organization, and so forth may be completely different. This helps explain why organizations that succeed in bringing disruptive technology to the marketplace often replace the organizations offering the older technology. Even if the older organizations can offer the newer technology, they often cannot make the changes to their business model necessary to succeed with it.

Disruptive Competition

Disruptive competition is similar to disruptive technology, but represents a difference in business models and not necessarily a product or technology. For example, Starbuck's coffee is not different technologically from other coffees, but their business model is quite different. Starbuck's chose not to compete on low price; their coffee is substantially more expensive than their older, more traditional competitors. They chose to have a unique sort of flavor, much more dark and rich than a typical North American coffeeshop. They also chose to have informal, lounge style settings, as opposed to tables and chairs or booths. Nothing about Starbuck's required patents or new technology. They simply chose to compete in a different way.

Wal-Mart has excellent technology to control inventory and supplier relationships, but it is their business model more than their technology that makes them a threat to other retailers. Any retailer could have bought the same computers and software as Wal-Mart. Their buildings required no new technology, and other than having higher ceilings than the buildings of older discount retailers (making them lighter, more attractive, and able to hold more inventory) they are basically the same as those of their competitors. Everyday low prices as opposed to sales, coupons, and specials are not new technology, but it was a unique way of doing business. Wal-Mart may not possess new technology, but their business model has certainly proven disruptive to retailers across the world.

Initially, McDonald's grew thanks largely to quick service, which at one time was quite unique. At the time that McDonald's first came on the scene, travelers would joke other restaurants must have trained their staff specially to be slow, so they couldn't get jobs anywhere else. People in a hurry (commonly known as everyone) didn't take long to gravitate to McDonald's.

Disruptive competitors often have different cost structures, different delivery methodologies, and different organizational hierarchies than their competitors. Another example is wholesale clubs, which charge people to become members before they can buy, only offer a narrow range of selection, and sell most products only in bulk quantities.

Disruptive competitors often accompany or are facilitated by a disruptive technology, but that is not required. Disruptive competition tends to use technology in a different way. Generally speaking, the type of technology available to organizations like Wal-Mart is the same as that available to organizations like K-Mart. Any restaurateur could have purchased the same equipment as McDonald's, most simply chose not to do so.

The advent of better ways to communicate and travel helped give rise to new groups of competitors. Better roads, better telephones, and computerized inventory made it possible for Wal-Mart to replace many small-town stores.

"Big box" stores, like Home Depot and Office Max, have proven to be disruptive competition for small mom-and-pop hardware stores and office supply stores. Such small stores have often disappeared after the big box competitors arrive. Technologically, there is nothing new about making a really big hardware store or a really big office supply store. However, their effect has been to drive smaller competitors out of the market.

Disruptive Marketplace

A *disruptive marketplace* is not a single competitor or even a group of competitors, but an environmental change that alters the way people can do business.

A disruptive marketplace threatens to change business models for all buyers and sellers. Television and radio made it possible for companies like Procter & Gamble to succeed with mass brand advertising. Commodity and securities markets were and still are being completely revamped through opportunities brought about by the Internet.

Just as radio and television each contributed to major changes and new opportunities for all kinds of buyers and sellers, the Internet is fostering many disruptive marketplaces for consumers and businesses.

If you work in newspapers, radio, or television, you probably view the Internet as disruptive technology. However, if you have an antique collectable store, you probably view it as a disruptive marketplace.

A disruptive marketplace dramatically lowers costs or barriers to information. The fact that consumers can gather mortgage rate information for free from multiple lenders before applying for a mortgage changes the way business is done, even if they decide to borrow from their local bank.

Sites that allow consumers to exchange and download music threaten many business models in entertainment. Discount selling and direct selling of airline tickets and easier access to information about destinations via the Internet has had a great impact on travel agents, forcing many out of business.

Web auctions, through sites such as eBay, have helped define the marketplace for a myriad of obscure items. In addition, eBay is replacing more traditional forms of media as an advertising space. For example, there are fewer collector cars advertised in newspapers and magazines, because they are being offered on eBay instead.

A disruptive marketplace can create new business models, like the way thousands of people can now make their living selling through Internet auctions. It can change old business models, like it has for travel agents. It is beyond the control of any one company and forces all companies to adapt.

The Importance of Management Push

Gathering better information with the intention to help an organization to do the same things better often indicates that the organization should instead be doing different things.

Overcoming hysteresis and internal adoption hurdles requires the support, facilitation, and directive of top management. Organizations tend to change infrequently and seldom in small increments. It is crucial to guide the process from the top, to make sure changes happen at the right time and in the right direction.

Consider the Sprint PCS example. It directly competes in the core market of the long distance and local divisions. However, if top management had not created Sprint PCS as a separate division, Sprint as a whole would probably be out of business or have been taken over by a competitor by now. Sprint PCS could not have grown organically out of any of the older sister divisions; it required a major management effort to create.

Dealing with change involves making a serious assessment of outside threats and internal opportunities. Some of the outside threats, particularly disruptive technology, may be harder to spot and even harder to get the organization to take advantage of. By the time everyone sees the need for change, it is usually too late. Management must not only see the need early on, but act upon it as well.

Changing strategic direction requires change in how the organization is arranged. Allowing people to stay in their comfort zone is rarely the way to success. To a great extent, top management needs to create enough discomfort within the organization to move it from where it is to where it needs to be.

Obstacles to Change

There are a variety of obstacles that organizations may encounter and must overcome to initiate the necessary changes in their business model.

Pressure for Immediate Success

One of the natural impediments to making strategic changes is the pressure for immediate success. Strategic change is by nature longer-term (as opposed to shorter-term tactical change) and learning often grows out of failures. Yet investors, employees, and customers like to see immediate results. It is important to convey the time results will take, and to expect and allow for some degree of changes along the way.

An inherent challenge to making long-term changes is that failure in the short-term makes success more difficult. While even small failures may bruise the pride of some, larger failures weaken the position of the organization financially. The paradox is that in order to make effective changes, some degree of experimentation is required. Naturally, some experiments will fail. The ability to learn quickly is crucial to successful change management.

For example, an organization building a CRM system costing in excess of $1 million took several years to prepare the system for implementation. They found the inevitable problems with the system were ripe targets for people threatened by the system.

When the system was rolled out company-wide, they then found that people didn't want to use it. The clerks didn't capture the information about the customer at the point-of-sale and the salespeople wouldn't use the system at all. On top of that, the old methods of tracking customers were discontinued when the new system was installed because the cost of the new system was so great the company didn't think they could justify keeping the old system.

It took well over a year to partially fix the new system by modifying how the clerks entered data, changing how their performance was measured, and holding managers responsible. However, after two years and counting, the salespeople still don't use the system.

Another approach would be to start with smaller, pilot programs where possible. Learn as you go, even if it is learning the hard way, and demonstrate how the project will benefit the company before undertaking a major implementation. Always remember the old rule, "if you can't do it manually, you can't automate it."

Organization Charts Reflect Strategy

An organization chart reveals how an organization does business. It becomes obvious by looking at an organization chart to know if an organization is a manufacturer or a service firm, and whether it is marketing-driven, or whether it is product-focused.

The organization chart should reveal what an enterprise's strengths, weaknesses, and methods of creating rewards and measures are likely to be. The chain-of-command should be clear and how the company adds value should be obvious.

Organization charts are created to reflect strategy, though they often lag behind intentions. It is usually a good starting place when trying to understand strategy, but will likely need to change when strategy changes.

Consider the following two examples of organization charts:

Exhibit 8.2: Manufacturing Organization Chart

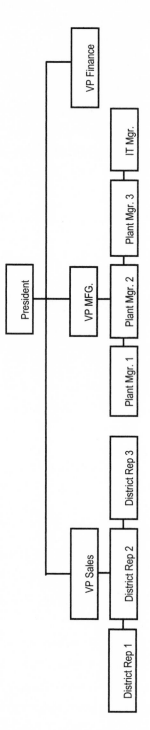

Exhibit 8.3: Sales and Distribution Organization Chart

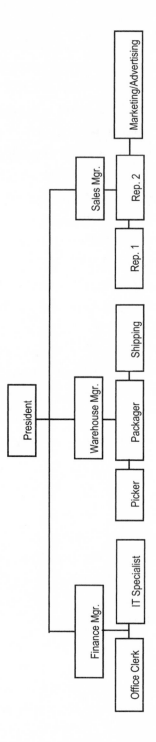

Notice that by simply looking at the charts, you can see that Exhibit 8.2 is a manufacturing firm and Exhibit 8.3 is a sales and distribution organization. Both organizations are aligned around their core mission and built to pursue a certain strategy in line with the mission.

In the example of the manufacturing firm, the IT resources belong to manufacturing. This is common for most manufacturers, who at best integrate manufacturing and accounting. This usually presents a challenge for the VP of Sales, as she has no IT resources and doesn't stand on equal footing with manufacturing for system needs.

In Exhibit 8.3, the sales and distribution example, the marketing and advertising rep is under the Sales Manager, and the IT specialist is under the Finance Manager. It would be a nearly impossible challenge for the marketer to build a data-driven integrated marketing campaign without major changes to the organization or without complete support from the Finance Manager.

Here is an example of how this affects what managers can and cannot accomplish. A marketing manager working for a manufacturing firm found that there were a large number of companies that did some business with the organization, but they were just like their bigger customers. The company had nearly 50 field sales reps, but they were too busy with their existing larger clients. So, the marketing manager wanted to build a campaign to contact each of them by mail and phone, and follow-up on a regular basis.

The campaign would start by calling each of the companies, which would be assigned to a telesales rep. The problem, however, was that there was only one person in the whole company who made out-bound calls, and that person worked mainly on service issues. Given the number of potential targets, the marketing manager needed about a dozen people to make calls.

The sales reps and sales manager didn't want the company to create a new department that might compete with them. Top management didn't want to hire new people. IT didn't want to create a new system to support a telesales department and didn't want an outside vendor either.

The idea died a very quick death, despite high expectations and a high expected return on investment.

Organization charts show the formal structure of the organization, but the informal structure can be just as important. Informal structure is sometimes more important to understand than formal structure. Power is often hidden in obscure places.

Notice in the manufacturing example that finance is off by itself. Neither sales nor manufacturing are a direct report to finance. This is usually a situation where a person or department has a large degree of informal power. They control resources that are important to many non-direct reporting people.

It is safe to assume that no major changes are made bottom-up without the consent or buy-in of people with informal power. They can make or break the case with top managers, and often act as gatekeepers to top management. The direct-reporting structure of the organization chart is how the company says it is organized, but the people with indirect control often prove that their informal structure is how the company actually functions.

The following example (Exhibit 8.4) from NASA helps illustrate where informal structure is likely to play a role.

Notice that there are no fewer that seven departments between the director and the departments that actually do the space flights. None of these seven really perform the mission of NASA, but each of them is capable of stopping any project dead in its track.

For example, Safety and Mission Assurance can change what the Space Shuttle Projects department is doing at any time. This is probably a good thing, but does add to the number of layers that must approve any major change.

The Office of the Chief Counsel (the legal department) is another area with large amounts of informal power. Other managers don't report directly to them, but their buy-in is crucial.

Departments that share computer systems tend to have stronger bonds than departments that do not. For example, if finance/accounting and manufacturing share the same system while sales and marketing are

Exhibit 8.4: NASA Organization Chart

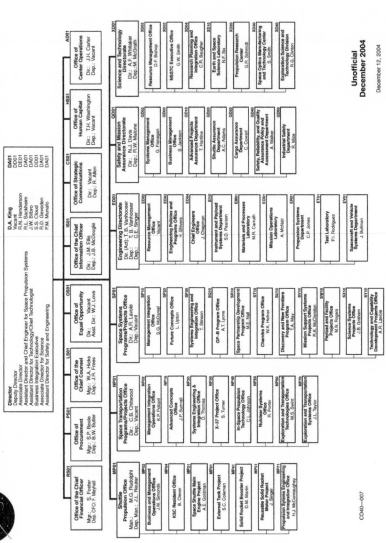

MSFC Organizational Chart

Director
Deputy Director
Associate Director
Assistant Director and Chief Engineer for Space Propulsion Systems
Assistant Director for Technology/Chief Technologist
Business Integration Executive
Associate Director for Science
Assistant Director for Safety and Engineering

D.A. King — DA01
Vacant — DD01
R.N. Henderson — DE01
R.L. Sackheim — DA01
J.W. Bibro — DA01
S.S. Cloud — DA01
R.D. Geveden — DD01
P.M. Munafo — DA01

Office of the Chief Financial Officer — RS01
Mgr.: S. Foster
Dep. CFO: F. Mayhall

Office of Procurement — PS01
Mgr.: S.P. Beale
Dep.: B.W. Butler

Office of the Chief Counsel — LS01
Mgr.: W.A. Hicks
Dep.: J.R. Froes

Office of Equal Opportunity — OS01
Dir.: Vacant
Asst. Dir.: W.J. Lowe

Office of the Chief Information Officer — IS01
Dir.: A.F. Whitaker
Dep.: J.B. McDougle

Office of Strategic Communications — CS01
Dir.: Vacant
Dep.: R. Allen

Office of Human Capital — HS01
Dir.: T.H. Washington
Dep.: Vacant

Office of Center Operations — AD01
Dir.: J.H. Carter
Dep.: Vacant

Shuttle Propulsion Office — MP01
Man.: M.G. Rudolphi
Dep. Man.: J.L. Reuter

- Business and Management Operations Office — MP02
  J.M. Simonds
- KSC Resident Office — MP04
  B. Oliver
- Space Shuttle Main Engine Project — MP20
  A.E. Goldman
- External Tank Project — MP31
  S.C. Coleman
- Solid Rocket Booster Project — MP41
  C.I. Johnson
- Reusable Solid Rocket Motor Project — MP51
  J. Singer
- Propulsion Systems Engineering and Integration Office — MP71
  H.J. McConnaughey

Space Transportation Programs/Projects Office — NP01
Dir.: C.B. Chitwood
Dep.: Vacant

- Management Integration Operations Office — NP02
  K.P. Pollard
- Advanced Concepts Office — NP04
  J.P. Sumrall
- Systems Engineering & Integration Office — NP20
  D. Thomas
- X-37 Project Office — NP30
  S. Turner
- In-Space Propulsion Technology Office — NP40
  R. Porter
- Nuclear Systems Office — NP50
  R. Porter
- Exploration and Transportation Technologies Office — NP90
  J.L. Taylor

Space Systems Programs/Projects Office — SP01
Dir.: A.R. Lavoie
Dep.: Vacant

- Management Integration Office — SP10
  S.S. McDaniel
- Future Concepts Office — SP20
  L. Upton
- Systems Engineering and Integration Office — SQ10
  T. Stinson
- GP-B Program Office — SR10
  A.T. Lyons
- Space Partnership Development Program Office — SR70
  M.E. Nall
- Chandra Program Office — ST10
  W.K. Hefner
- Discovery and New Frontiers Program Office — SV10
  T.A. May
- Mission Support Systems Projects Office — SW10
  R.K. McClendon
- Payload and Facility Projects Office — SW70
  M.N. Rogers
- Science Systems Projects Office — SX10
  J.B. Graham
- Technology and Capability Development Projects Office — SY10
  A.R. Lavoie

Engineering Directorate — ED01
Dir. (Act): T.B. Vanhooser
Dep.: C.B. Vanhooser
Dep.: G.E. Singer

- Resource Management Office — ED02
  Vacant
- Engineering Policies and Programs Office — ED04
  H. Stevens
- Chief Engineers Office — ED10
  J. Chapman
- Instrument and Payload Systems Department — ET10
  S.D. Pearson
- Materials and Processes Laboratory — EM01
  M.R. Carruth
- Mission Operations Laboratory — EO01
  A. McNair
- Propulsion Systems Department — ER01
  C.P. Jones
- Test Laboratory — ET01
  P.I. Rodriguez
- Spacecraft and Vehicle Systems Department — EV01
  J. Bulfman

Safety and Mission Assurance Directorate — CD01
Dir.: N.J. Davis
Dep.: R.W. Malone

- Systems Management Office — QD02
  G. Flanagan
- Business Management Office — QD04
  S. Jackson
- Advanced Projects Assurance Department — QD10
  T. Hartline
- Shuttle Assurance Department — QD20
  A.C. Adams
- Cargo Assurance Department — QD30
  C. Cowart
- Safety, Reliability, and Quality Assurance Policy and Assessment Department — QD40
  A. Walker
- Industrial Safety Department — QD50
  R. Mize

Science and Technology Directorate — XD01
Dir.: A.F. Whitaker
Dep.: M. McGrath

- Resource Management Office — XD02
  D.F. Bishop
- NSSTC Executive Office — XD03
  G.W. Smith
- Research Planning and Integration Office — XD04
  C.R. Raugher
- Earth and Space Science Laboratory — XD10
  N.F. Six
- Propulsion Research Center — XD20
  G.R. Schmidt
- Space Optics Manufacturing and Technology Center — XD30
  S. Smith
- Exploration Science and Technology Division — XD40
  R.G. Clinton

CD40—007

George C. Marshall Space Flight Center

Unofficial
December 2004

December 12, 2004

Source: National Aeronautics and Space Administration, Marshall Space Flight Center, Huntsville, Alabama.
http://ohc.msfc.nasa.gov/eso/charts/index.html

separate, there is probably a greater degree of informal cooperation among finance/accounting and manufacturing than there is among finance/accounting and sales.

It becomes obvious quickly that if you can't change the organization chart, you can't drive strategy. Top managers have to step in and change the organizational structure in order for some changes to occur at all.

Managing Rewards and Measurements

Changing rewards and measurements is threatening to employees and not something that can be readily or easily changed again once put in place. As a long-term strategic component, it is a crucial, but difficult tool to manage for a short-term tactical focus. Considering how rewards and measurements will need to change should be a part of long- and medium-term strategy to be sure that careful planning and thought is behind each change.

Before setting out to change strategy or build a new business model, managers need to accept the fact they will have to change rewards and measurements. Without modifications in these areas, change efforts are nearly always doomed before they start.

For example, a company manufactures components that are used for heating, temperature sensing, and controlling temperature. Heating components are made in one plant, sensing components are made in another plant, and controls are made in a third plant.

Upon reviewing their data, it was discovered that very few customers bought all three or even two types of components from the company. Most customers bought only one type of component, even though all three tend to be needed together.

As it turned out, salespeople worked for each plant and not a central sales department. The salespeople from one plant had no reason to work with the salespeople from the other plants. Salespeople could not sell components from other plants and got no reward for working with salespeople in the other plants. Each plant did their own marketing, and rather then viewing the other plants as a cross-sell opportunity, they viewed each other as competition. Knowing that, it made perfect sense that few customers bought more than one type of component from them.

Caterpillar truck engines used to be the number three truck engine manufacturer in the U.S., but worked their way up to number one. Part of the reason for this is how they changed the sales structure to support their desire to grow.

In order to become number one, Caterpillar needed to convert many prospective truck fleets into buyers. Most of their customers in the past were owner-operators and smaller companies that owned only a few trucks. Since the salespeople made money more easily by selling to existing customers, Caterpillar created target acquisition accounts and paid the salespeople a higher commission when they made sales to the fleets they had targeted.

As a result, salespeople could afford to spend the time going after potential new customers, knowing the target customers were more likely to become good customers, and knowing they would get a higher commission than from other accounts. The resulting change in market position demonstrates the effectiveness of the change.

Most people do what they are paid to do, and methods for judging employee performance and rewarding desired behavior should reflect that fact. New rewards and measurements must support change efforts, such as a major change in strategy that requires new jobs and new tasks. Otherwise, people will have no incentive to change, preferring and being rewarded for doing things in the same old way.

Agents of Change Versus Agents of Inertia

People in an organization will tend to actively or passively or openly or covertly align for or against change. Fortunately, not everyone will simply use "we've always done it this way" as a serious response to "why can't it be done differently?" Determining early on who is interested in change and who prefers to thwart it are crucial skills for managers and leaders.

There is a natural departmental bias against change that often takes managers by surprise. For example, human resources (HR) is often the department top management turns to when major changes in the work-force, such as layoffs, are deemed necessary. But turn that around for a moment, and look at it from an HR perspective. Wouldn't it be easier to keep people where they are? Won't the most difficult tasks fall to HR if there are major changes?

Consider the IT department, which is often a major resource for strategic change efforts. This department is very good at supporting well-defined, tactical needs with stable systems. When needs are loosely defined or system needs are changing drastically, support is much harder to deliver. The IT department will certainly want new systems that make IT more efficient, but they may balk at system changes that add work and uncertainty to IT.

For example, a business-to-business seller of food processing equipment built a new CRM system and then relied on their IT manager to put data into the CRM system for marketing to use.

Marketing gathered customer and transaction data, as well as infor-mation from Dun & Bradstreet about each customer, showing the cus-tomer company's size, type of business, sales volume, and so on.

The CRM system was not easy for IT to input data into and the IT manager couldn't understand why marketing needed the data. Rather than say, "No, I won't put the data into the CRM system," the IT man-ager would say, "I can't understand why marketing needs this data."

After two years, the CRM system, which cost many thousands of dol-lars, remains unloaded and unused. Top management never directed IT to load the system. They viewed it as a squabble among managers and let the system die.

The sales department may be viewed as one wanting change in the form of growth. But try to make a dramatic change in the price point of what is being sold, the delivery channel, or—heaven forbid—the com-mission structure and see what happens.

For example, a major trucking company found that its salespeople tended to spend their time calling only on their largest accounts, and spent little or no time with smaller accounts. The company concluded that having telesalespeople work directly with the smaller accounts would greatly improve business by giving accounts that were otherwise ignored some much needed attention.

The salespeople in the field were paid commission based on sales in their territory. The company wanted to give commission to the telesalespeople who called on the smaller accounts. Field sales did not want to give up any of their commission, whether the efforts from telesales resulted in more business or not.

Field sales had enough power in the company to win the argument. The company created the telesales department, but continued to pay full commission to the field sales reps on sales made by the telesales department. As a result, the cost advantage of calling on smaller accounts via telesales was greatly reduced and the company's financial ability to sell to smaller accounts was greatly diminished.

The fact that there will be winners and losers among departments resulting from strategic change is predictable. What is not always predictable is which individuals, regardless of department, will become agents of change and which will become agents of inertia. Particularly when top management is not willing to force needed change, good ideas are likely to die.

Knowledge of the Business of the Enterprise Is Key

Reaching for outside assistance, whether in consulting, analysis, or developing strategy, is a natural inclination for some managers. An outsider with an unbiased viewpoint can fulfill some roles, but the crucial roles that *must* be supported internally often are overlooked.

Particularly when dealing with data recorded in various systems, insider knowledge is key. How a company determines profit margins by sale may not be clear (it may not even be recorded). Which data fields have data that are used regularly and deemed accurate and which are seldom or never used are examples of things that must be sleuthed out within the organization. The on-the-ground, insider information is crucial to making reasonable interpretations.

Sometimes the understanding of data in a system doesn't come from the people who maintain it, but from the people who use it. They know what data can't be relied on and what data are accurate. As a basis for accurate analyses, systems usually have features and capacity for some types of reports or data that are never used and knowing what can't be trusted is as important as knowing what can be trusted. For example, a company that manufactured cellular phone components was organized into two divisions, one selling analog equipment and one selling digital equipment. Both wanted to market separately.

Upon reviewing their data, an analyst found about 80 percent of the company's customers that bought analog also bought digital. Then the analyst discovered 100 percent of the customer companies that bought digital also bought analog. So, the analyst did the logical thing and called the manufacturer to say there was something wrong with the data. Apparently, the analyst assumed, they had only sent digital customer data when those customers had also bought analog.

As it turned out, there was no mistake. Cellular phones may be digital phones, but they still require an analog microphone and speaker to be useful. People speak with each other in analog. It didn't take long to conclude that analog and digital components should be marketed together.

In another example, an equipment manufacturer was creating a marketing database and noticed their best customers did not appear to be spending very much money. Clearly, something was wrong.

Upon reviewing the data, and checking with several different people who couldn't figure out what was wrong, someone in accounting found the misunderstanding. It turned out that leasing the equipment was the most profitable method of selling, but the sales database only captured the first lease payment. As a result, it appeared that the best customers were instead very small customers. It took several weeks for marketing to track down a person who understood the problem before they could fix the misunderstanding.

Outside consultants, technical expertise, and computer capacity are not enough to drive a successful business modeling effort. Outside help must have internal support across departments to uncover the facts. In much the same way a technically savvy IT department may think they can handle the task alone, a savvy consulting firm may also think it can handle the task alone. Neither is usually correct.

Most times, analysis to support business modeling does two things. It quantifies what insiders already know and it provides completely new insights. To put it another way, it clarifies existing thinking, while offering new ideas. To which degree either will occur cannot be predicted in advance.

Driving Change

When managers seek to drive fundamental changes in the business model, certain change strategies are most commonly employed. Some of the most typical are outlined below, along with the key factors for selecting the most appropriate strategy for the change that needs to be implemented.

Organic Growth

Organic growth is the expansion of talent or capabilities (not necessarily corporate size or employee numbers) relying primarily on current structure and employees. In order to be successful, it requires willingness on the part of employees to change their day-to-day roles, often in unforeseen ways.

Organic growth is often most successful when the initial spark for the changes comes from people within the organization. Some of the considerations for top managers include:

- Does this group have the right fundamental skills to make these changes? For example, does having a degree and experience in computer science make someone a good choice for determining marketing strategy? Does experience in sales make someone a good choice for developing a highly technical product? Having the vision for change is one thing, being able to carry it out is another.

- Is the change simply a power play? People in IT, accounting, finance, and many other areas fully understand that knowledge is power. Of course, IT wants to control any new knowledge-delivery system, as does accounting, and finance. Keep in mind that knowledge systems should ultimately be controlled by people who make decisions based on that knowledge, not by the day-to-day caretakers who manage the technical aspects of the system.

- Are these people builders or managers? It is one thing to fly an airplane, it is quite another to design and build one. Managing a department is quite different from creating or re-creating a new department. It may require one set of managers to make major changes and another set to administer the departments once the changes are made.

Partnering

Partnering is the expansion of talent or capabilities through the creation of a business model allied with one or more outside organizations. In order to be successful, it requires the cooperation of a separate organization, which may need to feel safe from competition (i.e., being "cut out" later) or take-over.

Partnering can be very successful when key skill sets lie outside the organization. Some of the considerations for top managers include:

- Is speed of implementation crucial? If a partner is ready and willing, the changes can sometimes be made very quickly, without having to go through a lengthy buy-out discussion or internal restructuring. It may also be possible to carry out changes quietly, before competitors can react.

- Is there a complementary product or service that customers use along with current offerings? If the end-customer can combine purchases into a single, attractive package, it may make both offerings more attractive.

- Is there a facilitator or market-maker available? A lender, leasing company, sales agent, or promoter may be able to fundamentally change the way some customers view their relationship with the organization. For example, many retailers are supplied with store credit card programs by outside banks. Consider the effect companies like Amazon .com have had on publishers.

Acquisition

Acquisition is the expansion of talent or capabilities through the purchase of one or more outside organizations. In order to be successful, it requires many of the same things as partnering does, with the addition of a few more. The rules that apply to partnering and acquisition tend to apply to mergers as well.

Acquisition can be very successful when key skill sets outside the organization are crucial to future success. Some of the considerations for top managers include:

- Can it be bought at all? This is not the same question as whether or not it is for sale, but rather can what is being bought be kept, managed, and controlled? For example, buying a law firm without guarantees the attorneys will remain would be a waste if (or when) those attorneys leave to find or form another organization.
- Is it affordable? Does the organization have the financial means to make the purchase and is the purchase a good value?
- Can it be integrated into the organization? While it may be a good value to put resources into an investment that is an autonomous business model, it may not benefit the core business.

Creating a Subsidiary

Acquisition is the expansion of talent or capabilities through the building of a new organization, separate from the original, with a distinctly different business model. It may be radical organic growth, where a new group is split off from the old, and it may contain some talents that are acquired.

Creating a subsidiary can be successful when the new business model can stand on its own, the parent company can afford to split off the new group, and the corporate culture of the old group is not made into a burden for the new. Some considerations for top managers include:

- Does the culture of the existing organization prevent making the changes required to give the new effort a fighting chance? For example, General Motors had to create Saturn in order to have a dealer network that would sell the product in a new way.
- Does the economics of the existing business model prevent the new business model from succeeding in the current environment? A company selling high-cost, high-margin items through field sales reps may not be able to sell a low-margin, high-volume item. Consider IBM's failure to sell PCs using its mainframe sales practices.
- Is there a long-term payoff in starting a subsidiary, beyond investment return? A subsidiary developing disruptive technology may represent a long-term survival strategy, by making sure the organization as a whole won't be displaced by new technology.

Divestment

Divestment (spin-off) is the expansion of talent or capabilities through the building of a new organization, separate from the original, with a distinctly different business model, which is sold to provide funds for the parent organization. Divestment often becomes an option in situations similar to those favoring the creation of a subsidiary.

Divestment is an option when the parent company cannot fully develop a new business model or other parties can build more value into the new organization. Sometimes, small ventures are sold to insiders who might otherwise simply leave and take their intellectual capital with them. Some considerations for top managers include:

- Is there a risk of key people leaving on their own and destroying the value to the parent company? Selling some or the entire new venture to insiders may be an option.
- Would other companies value the new venture more highly than the parent? If so, it may be most profitable to sell it.
- Will the new venture become a threat to the parent? If so, it may make more sense to create a subsidiary and/or partner to retain control of the new organization.

Specialization

Specialization is the contraction of talent or capabilities through the simplification of the organization, resulting in a new business model. Rather than separating or selling a division, the organization simply stops doing things it isn't good at. Specialization is sometimes the result of a failed attempt to diversify. It is used in circumstances similar to both divestment and creating a subsidiary.

Specialization is an option when divisions, products, services, or outlets are not providing enough value to operate at a profit, and cannot be sold or split off. Some considerations for top managers include:

- Is the product or service necessary for the business as a whole? For example, a chain of burger restaurants made a major effort to sell fried chicken, but after it proved unsuccessful, they simply dropped it. It was not necessary to their core business of selling burger meals.
- Do the extra capabilities distract from the core competencies? Does quality, service, or customer focus suffer as a

result of too many job functions? As they say, if you have
more than three priorities, you don't have any.

- Is it neither a profit center nor something that can be sold?
Even if the organization may be able to sell equipment that
is no longer needed, it may be impossible to sell the capabilities as an on-going venture.

New Media Channels

Adding new media channels results is the expansion of talent or capabilities by communicating with customers or suppliers via new means, resulting in a new business model. It may be a subtle change, such as a
direct-mail cataloger advertising in newspapers or a more fundamental
change, such as moving telephone customer service to a website.

New media channels represent an option that is often ignored or
under-utilized. On the other hand, many organizations have been caught
in the rush to create a website, without considering the impact on their
business model. Some considerations for top managers include:

- Do the new media have the potential to add value or lower
cost to the relationship? For example, will having a telesales department in addition to field sales allow customers
needing quick answers or making smaller purchases to
have a smoother relationship than those who must wait to
see a sales rep in person (or track down someone who is always traveling)?
- Is the fixed cost of trying a new media channel low enough
to make a test worthwhile? For example, many direct mailers have successfully used infomercials, but only in cases
where the cost of creating infomercials was justified by potential sales volume.
- Have new media been tested in the past? In a case where an

organization has stuck to only one or a few media, it can often find through testing that other media are quite effective.

New Sales Channels

Adding new sales or distribution channels results in the expansion of talent or capabilities by selling to customers via new means, which results in a new business model. It may be as small as adding a new response mechanism, such as a restaurant taking fax orders or as big as a retailer adding a direct-mail catalog.

A website may be a new sales channel or it may simply be a new media channel. New sales channels typically result in some customers buying more (due to the greater convenience of having more options) and gaining new customers attracted by the new channel. Some considerations for top managers include:

- Are there potential customers who would likely consider buying if a new sales channel were available? For example, are there people who would buy the product if it was at a local retail store, such as an Eddie Bauer store, who would not buy from the Eddie Bauer catalog?
- Will the convenience of a new sales channel encourage customers to buy more or buy more often? For example, will companies that have ordered lunch for their office by phone occasionally order more often or make larger orders if they can fax the order instead?
- Does the new sales channel offer better economics—at least for some customers—than current channels? In other words, is the relationship a better deal either because of better pricing, better service and convenience, or lower fulfillment costs?

New Constituent Relationships

Changing or adding a constituent relationship results in a different deployment of talent or effort within the organization, but not necessarily an expansion or contraction.

A *constituent* is any person or firm in the organization's environment that can materially affect its ability to function. An example would be government regulation of product safety. Those who support and implement the regulation may not be in the seller-buyer chain, but can affect it nonetheless.

Constituent relationships are the most often ignored and undervalued. Constituents may have a positive effect on sales, for example the way Mustang clubs spur sales of new Ford cars. By the same token they can have negative effects. For example, people concerned with vehicle fuel economy were hostile toward the Ford Excursion and played a role in that vehicle going out of production.

Traditionally, the management of constituent relationships was best understood by non-profit organizations, but for-profit businesses increasingly realize that it entails more than just PR. Some considerations for top managers include:

- Is the sales process affected by influencers? For example, pharmaceutical companies realize that doctors must prescribe a medication before a consumer can buy it.
- Does the organization have a major impact on the environment? This can be either social or environmental. For example, automobiles have a major impact in both areas. In such cases, consumer groups and regulators are important constituents, as are those who plan, build, and maintain roads.
- Is the product or service used on behalf of others? A non-profit group may serve one group, but be funded by a dif-

ferent or several, other groups. Each group should see the value in the relationship.

Consummating the Sale

Changing how a product or service can be paid for can have a major impact on the business model. Goods and services are quite often not simply sold for cash. Renting, leasing, credit cards, and store charge accounts with their low-interest offers can greatly affect not only how much is sold, but who can and will buy.

How sales are consummated is changing rapidly with technology and future changes are often feared even when they offer an opportunity. Consider how the movie industry feared video rentals and now finds them a major profit center or how the video rental industry, in order to cope with customer complaints over late fees, went from pay-per-rental to monthly fees where customers could exchange videos when it was convenient for them. Some considerations for top managers include:

- Is technology changing the delivery or availability of the product or service? For example, the Internet and wireless phone plans have radically change how people look at long-distance phone service, and have affected how they are willing to pay for it.
- Would a different method of payment broaden the market? Fewer videos would be sold if they could not be rented and fewer cars would be "sold" if they were not made more affordable to some through leasing.
- Can a market-maker or facilitator supply a different mechanism to sell with? For example, will a bank or lending company supply a store with their own credit card so they can offer a six-months-same-as-cash as a promotional tool?

Pricing

Pricing can affect the business model in ways that are similar to changes in how a sale is consummated. There is far more to pricing than simply raising or lowering the price. For example, items can be bundled together and sold as a package. In some case, items are given free with a purchase; in other cases they are given as free samples in the hopes of driving future purchases.

Many businesses find they cannot afford to make small sales (when their transaction costs are too high) and are forced to either eliminate small items or sell them only in larger bundles. Airlines have developed sophisticated pricing models that adjust the prices of seats based on availability. Some considerations for top managers include:

- Has different pricing been tested? Many businesses create packages that are too cheap and consumers don't value them. Try selling three items for more, instead of one item for less.

- Does the first sale provide major revenue or minor revenue? Businesses often make a small purchase to try out a new service or supplier. Giving a free sample may be a better way to begin the relationship if future sales are likely to be large.

- Is the average sale profitable? Many times, businesses make money only on larger orders, when the cost to fulfill an order is considered. If the average sale is not profitable, can they be replaced by fewer but larger orders of similar total revenue?

A quick review of basic techniques to change the business model reveals that almost any change will invariably threaten someone's status quo. Trying too hard to avoid making any constituents upset or trying to avoid conflict among managers will often shut down the change process before it even starts. Keeping this in mind is important as you implement changes to your business model.

Case Studies

The four cases in this chapter provide examples of how data-driven techniques and applications discussed in this book were used to assess specific challenges and support needed changes in the strategic direction of each company.

The first three cases present the situation, the analysis, and the results for each company. The fourth case is longer and more detailed.

How Profiling Changed a Business Model

Situation

A Web-based firm created to sell goods and supplies to small office/home office (SOHO) firms with four or fewer employees was not growing at the pace they had expected. They had a convergent business model, selling many products through one channel, their website.

Order amounts ranged from very small to very large, occasionally exceeding $10,000. The mean average order was $500, but the median average order was less than $50. In fact, about 80 percent of orders were under $50. Given the large number of small orders, it seemed logical they were coming from small businesses.

They assumed the SOHOs would appreciate the convenience of

ordering online. This convenience, they thought, would give them an advantage over other companies' competitive business models, like the big-box office supply stores.

Seeking a better way to target their perceived market, they set about to do profiling, and see if their customer base looked like they expected. Customer names and purchases were used in the analysis. Being able to profile sales as well as customers proved crucial to the outcome, as we will see.

Analysis

Purchase behavior (orders, amount of order) was summarized by customer first; then the customers were overlaid with business demographics (firmagraphics) provided by a compiler.

The firmagraphic data included the following:

- SIC Code (Standard Industrial Classification Code, or "type of business")
- Number of Employees

There are thousands of SIC codes, and they found their customers were in many different industries, which was not surprising. As expected, customers were mostly white-collar rather than manufacturing firms. By percentage of their customer base, they found that their top five SIC Codes were:

- 7389 Business Services
- 7999 Miscellaneous Personal Services
- 6411 Insurance Agents, Brokers, and Services
- 8748 Business Consulting
- 8711 Engineering Services

Next, the company reviewed how many customers they had in each employee size range. Their percentage of customers by employee size range looked like Exhibit 9.1.

Exhibit 9.1: Percentage of Customers by Firm Employee Size Range

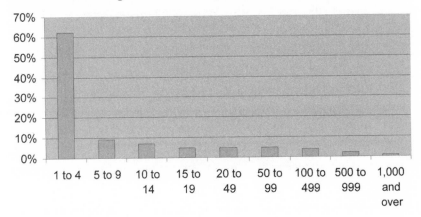

So far, so good. Based on the data they had analyzed to this point, everything seemed to be in line with their original expectations. Then they decided to look at percentage of sales by number of employees, which looked like Exhibit 9.2.

Exhibit 9.2: Percentage of Sales by Number of Employees

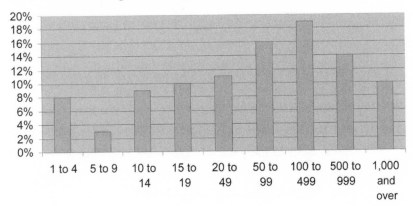

Results were dramatically different when viewed by sales. Their "target market" of SOHOs was only 8 percent of sales, despite being over 60 percent of customers. In fact, companies with 50 or more employees made up over half their sales.

In light of these results, they took a second look at sales by SIC Code. Not surprisingly, the top five SIC codes looked quite different, too.

- 6021   National Commercial Banks
- 5511   New and Used Car Dealers
- 8011   Offices and Clinics of Medical Doctors (hospitals)
- 5085   Industrial Machinery and Equipment
- 7311   Advertising Agencies

This caused the company to look at competitive and parallel business models serving SOHOs. They found the big-box stores, such as Office Max and Sam's Club, did a booming business with individuals and small businesses. It seemed SOHOs preferred to shop for themselves, but people in larger companies preferred the convenience of online purchasing.

Looking at their sales, they found the small businesses tended to buy once and leave. The larger companies bought again and again. Interestingly, they uncovered what they called the "$50 every two weeks" segment. This group tended to be in larger organizations, ordered about every two weeks, but never in amounts over $50. Further research revealed these customers were authorized to spend up to $50 whenever they needed to but had to get authorization to spend more. For them, being able to order one or two things they needed any time was a real convenience.

Looking at where their larger customers came from, they found that nearly all had been brought in by the company's owners and managers. Only a few came through the company's website. Unwittingly, they had run their company with two sales channels. The website, of course, was one channel, but in addition, they had acted like their own sales reps. Most of their business came about through their "informal" sales rep channel.

Results

The management reorganized the company to include sales reps calling on larger firms, in addition to selling on the Web. The website would still be used to take orders, but salespeople would find new customers among larger companies. Their convergent business model became a compound business model.

The key to making profiling so effective was looking not just at customers, but in looking at sales. The "average" or "typical" customer is often not profitable, and the 80/20 rule nearly always applies. To be useful, profiling should be directed toward the 20 percent of customers that bring in 80 percent of sales. It is then possible to adjust the business model to fit the most profitable customers.

How Cluster Analysis Changed a Business Model

Situation

American Wood Working manufactures several types of equipment, primarily scroll saws (which can cut detailed and intricate shapes). They also manufacture planers (which make wood a uniform thickness).

Theirs was a divergent business model. They manufactured machines, which they sold to hobbyists or small business through magazine ads, catalogs, and traveling sales reps. These sales reps can generally be found at any large woodworking show and occasionally at other large events, such as state fairs. The machines cost anywhere from $600 to several thousand dollars and can last many years. For a hobbyist they can last a lifetime.

American Wood Working assumed their market was men, primarily in their 50s, with a blue-collar background. These were the people they remembered from the woodworking shows, often with their arms full of "new toys" they'd just bought from other vendors.

Their goal was to find out what their customers "looked like" and to see if their ideas about their customers were really correct.

Analysis

Customer data were overlaid with consumer demographics and business firmagraphics. Customer data included which woodworking magazines they read, what other tools they owned, and what they made with their equipment.

Demographic data primarily included:

- Age
- Income
- Marital Status
- Children (number, age)
- Homeowner (Yes, No)

Quickly, they found very few customers matched business firmagraphics. Apparently, users of their equipment were either hobbyists or part-time businesspeople, making a few things out of their homes.

A dynamic cluster analysis showed they had five basic groups of customers, large enough to market to, but small enough to be sufficiently different. While they were mostly similar in marital status (most were married) and generally neither high nor low in income, they did vary in other important ways. The clusters were:

- Traditional Woodworkers. Men, average age of 53, income of $49,000/year, nearly all married, homeowners, with either no children at home or one older child. Most likely reads *Wood* magazine, and owns many different pieces of woodworking equipment. Mostly makes craft items and simple furniture projects.
- In it for the Grandkids. Men, average age of 72, income of $47,000/year, about 2/3 married (some widowed), homeowners, no children at home. Most likely reads *Wood* magazine and has relatively few pieces of woodworking equipment. Mostly makes child-oriented gift items.
- In it for the Furniture. Men, average age of 41, income of $76,000/year, mostly married, homeowners, with 1 or more children at home. Most likely reads *Fine Woodworking* magazine, and owns high-end woodworking equip-

ment. Mostly makes furniture, antique reproductions, and fine-quality objects.

- In it for the Money. Mostly men, average age of 34, income of $32,000 a year, mostly married, with younger children at home. About half are homeowners, the other half are renters. Most likely reads *Woodworker Magazine*, has a few other pieces of woodworking equipment. Mostly makes crafts and simple projects that they usually sell to other people at crafts shows, fairs, and the like.

- In it for the Art. Mostly women, average age of 35, income of $57,000 a year mostly married, with younger children at home. Nearly all homeowners. Most likely reads *Decorative Woodcrafts* magazine. Has little or no woodworking equipment, except for their scroll saw. Uses the scroll saw to cut out decorative shapes and then paints them.

American Wood Worker recognized the traditional woodworkers as their primary market, but were surprised to find out they actually amounted to less than a third of their customers. By cluster, their customers broke out as shown in Exhibit 9.3.

Exhibit 9.3: Customers by Clusters

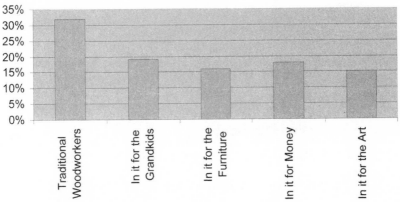

As it turned out, the company had a wide range of customers with a wide range of interests. This made them realize their customers must be using a very wide range of complementary products, including a variety of tools, patterns, designs, and even paints. This also pointed out that their marketing, geared entirely to men in their 50s doing simple projects, was off-target for many of their clusters.

Results

The analysis resulted in several immediate changes. First, they switched to a compound business model. They did this by gathering a variety of complementary merchandise from other manufacturers that they could sell to their own customers. They began sending a catalog to their customers, which included their own tools as well as complementary merchandise they knew their customers must be buying. Then, the company began including the complementary merchandise in their displays at woodworking shows. Sales were tracked carefully and it was found that the addition of complementary products increased overall sales without reducing sales of their own equipment.

In addition, American Wood Working revised its messages to each of its different audiences. For example, the previous ad in *Decorative Woodcrafts* magazine featured a man in his late 50s and did not mention cutting out shapes for painting. By changing the ad to feature a woman, and showing her woodwork and her painting, tripled response and sales coming from that magazine.

The company now has a broader offering, targeted differently to a wider array of channels. Sales have grown dramatically as a result.

How Profit-Based Segmentation Changed a Business Model

Situation

A manufacturer and supplier of electronic cellular telephone components offered several different product lines to manufacturers of complete wireless phones. They had three product lines that worked with analog data and two product lines that worked with digital data. Each product line had a different marketing manager and each manager wanted a separate catalog for each line.

The manufacturer tracked the contacts at each customer or prospect level by functional title, which was broken out into simple categories. Functional titles included:

- Sales/Marketing
- Production/Manufacturing
- Engineering/Design

The functional titles were used for two reasons. First, they assumed each area had a different responsibility regarding their products. Engineers would specify that their product should be used, sales or marketing would determine how many would be needed, and production would order them when needed. Secondly, they assumed different firms worked in different areas. A marketing firm would decide they needed a product with new features. They would hire engineers to design it and select a manufacturer to assemble it. The majority of their sales, it was assumed, came through different people at different firms, each with a different role in the sale, whether they actually made a purchase or not.

As such, they had a divergent business model. They manufactured their product, but sold it in different ways to different market segments. Given the complexities of the marketplace and the variety of experts needed to create a finished product like a cellular telephone, this approach seemed the most workable. However, marketing felt five separate catalogs for what seemed to the layman to be similar electronic components seemed excessive. Marketing also wondered if the assumption that companies that were not buying were actually "driving" the majority of sales was true. So, they set about to determine if actual customer behavior fit with their multi-dimensional approach to the market.

Exhibit 9.4: Percentage of Overall Sales by Functional Titles

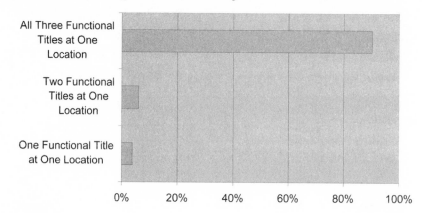

Analysis

One of the reasons given for such a segregated marketing approach was that each of the different functional titles is likely to be found at different firms. For example, one firm might be making purchases, perhaps a manufacturer, while other firms, perhaps an engineering consulting firm, was specifying which product should be used. If they ignored an engineering firm that does not buy, or buys only a few samples, the logic went, they could lose a very large amount of business if they stop specifying the product to manufacturers.

To test that hypothesis, they combined all the contacts by functional title with all the companies making purchases. They found that all large buyers and enough buyers to account for 90 percent of sales had contacts with all of the functional titles at their buying locations (Exhibit 9.4). In addition, the buyers tended to be well-known brand names that obviously had a full range of engineering, production, and marketing capabilities. True, there were a few independent engineers, mostly professors doing some consulting, but that affected only a small portion of sales.

Another reason justifying the segregated marketing approach was that some customers bought analog while others bought digital. In addition, customers tended to buy only one item number and not the full range. It was assumed that once they had designed a phone and specified the components that they would stay with those components for a while.

To test that hypothesis, the marketing department gathered all the sales at the transaction level and identified each product purchased by analog or digital and by product line within analog or digital. They summarized purchase behavior by customer to see if they did indeed tend to stay with one product line or if they preferred analog or digital. First, they looked at crossover within analog and digital, to see if customers bought one or more product lines of each type. They found the following:

Exhibit 9.5: Buyers of Analog Components

They found that only 20 percent of buyers of analog components bought only one product line. Clearly, that argued for at least a single analog catalog. Then they reviewed buyers of the two digital product lines, which looked like Exhibit 9.6.

Clearly, digital component buyers tended to buy both product families. That seemed to argue for a single digital catalog. At this point however, the analysis appeared to hit a snag. The data appeared incomplete. When they set out to review customer crossover among analog and digital component buyers, they arrived at the data indicated in Exhibit 9.7.

It appeared about 80 percent of analog buyers also bought digital components and ALL digital buyers bought analog. None of the digital buyers were digital only. The analyst naturally assumed that the data were incomplete. They must have sent only digital buyers that also

Exhibit 9.6: Buyers of Digital Components

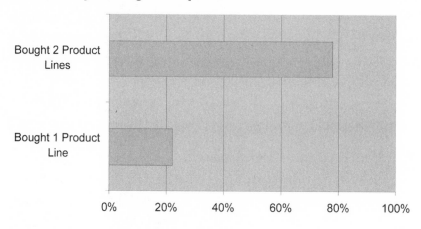

Exhibit 9.7: Digital and Analog Crossover

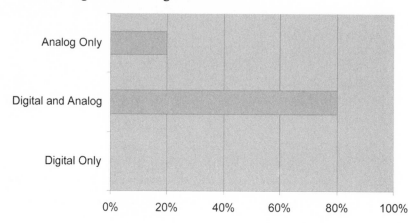

bought analog, so he called to explain the problem and ask for a more complete data set to fix the mistake.

However, there was no mistake. As it turns out, most cellular phones are digital. In this case, digital refers to how they communicate with the network. A few cellular phones, mostly older models, are analog. However, sound waves are analog. All telephones, whether digital or not, require analog speakers and microphones to work. Without them, people could not talk using cellular telephones. That is why 100 percent of digital buyers buy analog.

Results

Needless to say, the company now has one catalog featuring analog and digital components. In addition, they realized that segmenting the sales effort based on functional title made little sense, since the different areas of expertise tended to work together at the same location. Now, instead of a divergent business model they have a simple business model. A single sales rep is calling on each location, carrying one common catalog with all their products in it.

How Predicative Modeling Improved Subscription Marketing Effectiveness

Situation

A major U.S. symphony wanted to improve the effectiveness of its subscription marketing efforts. Traditionally, the symphony traded names with selected non-profits in its community. The traded lists are of ticket buyers, members, and donors from other organizations that sponsor such activities as opera, ballet, theatre, art exhibitions, and so forth.

In addition to trading lists, the symphony tested several lists based on demographics and psychographic lists. Some of these lists were based on clusters, some on demographic selects, and some on subscriptions. Demo names were always "ranked" behind trade names in the de-duplication process, so names on a demo were listed only on the demo list. Without exception, these names had performed poorly.

In total, the symphony traded with over 30 organizations and gathered over 500,000 trade names in addition to their own list of 250,000 past buyers and donors stretching back over ten years. Between their own patrons and the trade lists the predictive model identified fewer than 100,000 names worth contacting through direct marketing that are likely to purchase a subscription.

For simplicity, the case study will primarily detail a subscription campaign for the Classical series. The same techniques were applied to the other symphony products, such as Pops, Family, Donations, Single Tickets, Memberships, and so on.

Exchange Database Background

In 1993 a colleague and fellow direct marketing consultant asked the author to be a part of the marketing effort to support the local symphony. We experimented successfully with applying what were then basic direct marketing techniques. In an effort to improve responses to the various campaigns at the symphony, we partnered with a firm that specialized in creating selection models based primarily on demographic and lifestyle data. We found that using demographic and lifestyle segmentation was substantially better than using an un-segmented file. We used the model in several different cities, but found the model was best suited to the city where we created it, and not as effective in other areas.

Another finding was that behavior, such as whether or not someone had attended any performing arts events, was much more important than demographics. If someone had never been to the symphony, opera, ballet, or theater, it really didn't matter how old they were or how much income they had. Any time the behavior and demographics were compared, past behavior was always a better predictor of future behavior than were demographics or lifestyles.

Over time, we found what worked best and cost least was to encourage organizations to trade lists with as many other similar organizations as possible. The names were ranked by importance, de-duplicated, and the name inventory was created. It was cost-effective to create, gave the client organization a clear picture of who they had available to them to reach, and allowed for much better decisions regarding who should or should not be contacted.

Once a campaign was under way, results were matched to the name inventory. This showed response rates, average order, and so on. Over time, we learned which segments were likely to be most responsive. For example, we learned people on more than one list were most likely to respond than people on only one list, and that people who attended other performing arts events (e.g., opera, ballet, theatre) were more likely to attend the symphony than people who had joined only the zoo or subscribed to cultural magazines.

We discovered that sometimes results depended on how the list was de-duplicated. For example, if a symphony bought demographic or lifestyle names and the vendor ranked them "first" (ahead of the symphony ticket buyer names) then "demo" names would be credited with the responses from existing buyers. This happens when a name is on more than one list. The higher "ranked" name is kept, and the lower ranked name is "dupped-out."

Since behavior proved more important than demographics, we learned to rank "demo" names last. That way, the *only* names on a demo list after a merge/purge were unique, i.e., not on any other list. We found these names, whether they were based on a specific age/income select, lifestyle clusters, or any other kind of demographic/lifestyle segmentation produced little additional results. It was not uncommon to mail 10,000 or more "demo" names (not on any other list) and get less than $1,000 in sales from that list.

Eventually, the methods used most often were classic, catalog-style direct marketing. More recent activities, more frequent activities, and people on more than one list ("multi-buyers") responded best. In fact, we typically saw 80 percent of responses coming from the 20 percent of the list that were "multi-buyers" found on three or more lists.

"Multi-buyers" are clearly very important, so we set about to better understand them. Multi-buyers had simply been classified by the number of times they were found in the database, and not by the specific activities with which they had been involved. It seemed logical that someone who had been to the symphony three times was not the same as someone who had been a member of the zoo for three years. Yet according to the name inventory, they were both "multis." So, we set about to better understand this multi-buyer behavior.

In the process of developing a predictive model, we discovered a more effective way of segmenting the database, and a more efficient way of predicting who was likely to buy, donate, or attend than we had before. The following explains how the methodology works, starting with a more detailed description of the Name Inventory. The Name Inventory is the House File Inventory, plus the available "trade" (prospect) names the symphony intends to use but does not "own." The Name Inventory shows what happened to names that were put into the database.

The Source is listed, which corresponds to a specific activity or behavior. The sources are listed in RANK order (most to least estimated value). The example shown would be for a ticket marketing campaign.

The number of names INPUT is shown first, then "Infile Dupes." Infile Dupes are "true duplicates," or where the same name and address is shown more than once with the same Source.

A "House Dupe" is any name that is eliminated by a higher ranked "House" name. A House name is any name that came from the organization as opposed to a "Trade" name, which is any name from outside the organization doing the campaign. For example, a symphony ticket buyer is a House name for the symphony. An Art Museum name is a Trade name for the symphony.

Trade Dupes are shown next, which are names eliminated by another trade name. That is followed by Total Dupes, Bad Addresses (blank addresses or non-mailable), and then "Multi-Buyers," which are names on more than one list.

For example, if an 04 Single Ticket Buyer matches an Art Museum name, that Art Museum name is eliminated as a duplicate, and the 04 Single Ticket Buyer name becomes a Multi-Buyer.

Exhibit 9.8: Sample Inventory Report

Source	Input	Infile Dupes	House Dupe	Trade Dupe	Total Dupe	Bad Addresses	Multi-Buyers	Mail Output
04 Single Ticket Buyer	6,500	50	220		270	480	3,050	5,750
04 Special Event Ticket Buyer	800	20	25		45	25	420	730
03 Sampler Series Buyer	200	10	30		40	5	150	155
03 Single Ticket Buyer	10,500	75	550		625	1,300	3,975	8,575
03 Special Event Ticket Buyer	1,550	5	95		100	60	760	1,390
04 Prospect Responder	5,550	100	550		650	50	715	4,850
03 Prospect Responder	7,250	140	1,225		1,365	185	1,025	5,700
02 Prospect Responder	5,900	150	1,360		1,510	390	840	4,000
04 Donor	650	0	220		220	80	275	350
03 Donor	850	1	340		341	84	340	425
Art Museum	50,000	20	16,600	3,450	20,070	780	12,245	29,150
Opera	20,000	20	10,350	170	10,540	460	4,210	9,000
Theater	25,000	150	8,960	3,460	12,570	180	2,965	12,250
Ballet	8,000	10	1,417	670	2,097	303	975	5,600
	142,750	751	41,942	7,750	50,443	4,382	31,945	87,925

Mail Output is shown in the final column. Generally speaking, the bulk of responses come from Multi-Buyers and more recent House names.

Measuring Results Accurately

Measuring and understanding results was relatively simple when the campaign is managed using a Name Inventory. Results can be shown by segment, and experience with what does and doesn't work grew quickly. Of course, how the names were ranked does play a part, as described earlier in the discussion about Demo names.

As shown in Exhibit 9.9, 43 people responded to a subscription offer out of 33,488 people mailed. At an average mailing cost of under 50 cents each, that's not a bad return.

However, of the 43 responders, 12 were Multi-Buyers on exactly two lists, and 23 were on 3 or more lists. That's 36 of the 43 responders.

Of the 33,488 people mailed, 11,875 were Multi 3+ names. Multi 3+ names accounted for 35% of the mailing, and 53% of the response. Names that were not "Multi" accounted for 40% of the mailing, but only 19% of the response. The "Multi" names were profitable to contact, the "Non-Multi" names were not.

Exhibit 9.9: Name Inventory Report

Source	Number Contacted	# of Responders	Response Rate	Total $	Average Sales	$ per Contact
04 Single Ticket Buyer	4,719	20	0.42%	$18,791	939.55	3.98
04 Special Event Ticket Buyer	367	1	0.27%	-	-	-
03 Sampler Series Buyer	158	1	0.63%	$161	161.00	1.02
03 Single Ticket Buyer	6,562	8	0.12%	$5,302	662.75	0.81
03 Special Event Ticket Buyer	300	-			-	-
04 Prospect Responder	4,822	2	0.04%	$1,540	770.00	0.32
03 Prospect Responder	101				-	-
02 Prospect Responder	111	-			-	-
04 Donor	350	1	0.29%	$378	378.00	1.08
03 Donor	408	-				
Art Museum	4,200	1	0.02%	$720	720.00	0.17
Opera	8,797	7	0.08%	$2,692	384.57	0.31
Theater	2,073	1	0.05%	-	-	-
Ballet	520	1	0.19%	$650	650.00	1.25
TOTALS	**33,488**	**43**	**0.13%**	**$30,234**	**$ 703.12**	**$0.90**

Exhibit 9.10: Multi-Buyers Report

Source	Mailed Multi 2	Mailed Multi 3+	Responder Multi 2	Responder Multi 3+
04 Single Ticket Buyer	861	2,177	7	10
04 Special Event Ticket Buyer	82	161		
03 Sampler Series Buyer	20	127		1
03 Single Ticket Buyer	1,317	2,645	1	7
03 Special Event Ticket Buyer	43	257		
04 Prospect Responder	566	146	1	
03 Prospect Responder	3	98		
02 Prospect Responder	4	107		
04 Donor	29	245		
03 Donor	72	264		
Art Museum	1,830	2,370		1
Opera	2,035	2,173	2	4
Theater	1,131	893		
Ballet	305	212	1	
TOTALS	**8,298**	**11,875**	**12**	**23**

Exhibit 9.11: Modeled Segments Report

Node	Score	Number Contacted	# of Responders	Response Rate	Total $	Average Sales	$ per Contact
6	6.53	550	22	4.00%	15,492.00	704.18	28.17
22	4.96	531	6	1.13%	2,181.00	363.50	4.11
10	4.19	2,255	32	1.42%	21,895.00	684.22	9.71
16	3.23	365	3	0.82%	4,472.00	1,490.67	12.25

Selecting Multi-Buyers can be very effective. However, the segments created by the predictive model can be even more effective. Consider the results from a similar mailing using modeled segments.

As good as the Multi-Buyer selection was, the predictive model was more effective. The predictive model considered not only whether or not people were multi-buyers, it found distinctions among the multi-buyers.

While particularly effective at segmenting past buyer and donor names, it can also select "good" names out of a trade or outside list that might otherwise cost too much to target at all. For example, consider a list provided to the symphony from a ballet. Exhibit 9.12 indicates that 24 percent of the ballet names were selected for contact, but 76 percent were not.

Overall, the Ballet list would have roughly broken even. However, with the "good" names selected, it became profitable.

Exhibit 9.12: Ballet List Segment

▨ Ballet Selected   ■ Ballet Not Selected

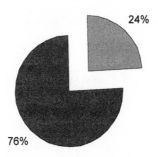

Exhibit 9.13: Theatre List Segment

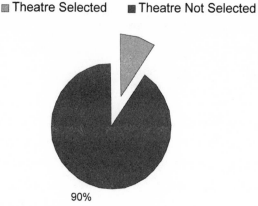

In the case of a Theatre list, only 10% of the names were selected. The Symphony would have lost money marketing to the Theatre list without this segmentation.

Because the predictive model did a good job of finding good names in marginal lists, fewer "good" prospects go without a contact. For example, the symphony mailed to fewer people in 2004 than 2003, but there were only 27 people who bought during the initial 2004 campaign that were from the non-mailed portion of the database, compared to 84 people in 2003. This demonstrates much better "good" names were selected from marginal segments. Despite targeting fewer people in 2004 than 2003, they still found fewer "non-targeted" people bought in 2004. The targets they selected were simply more on target.

To make the predictive model work, behavioral segments were coded into the database for the model to select as needed. They included:

- Single Ticket Buyer or Subscription Buyer for Classical, Pops, Jazz, Family, Holiday, and Other (a total of 12 categories for ticket buyers for this symphony)
- Prospects and Information Requestors
- Donors and Volunteers

The Symphony names were further coded based on Count (how many times they bought Classical Single Tickets), Recency (how long ago they bought Classical Single Tickets), and Amount (how much they donated or spent).

Trade name segments are grouped into categories, rather than simply one list source at a time. The categories include:

- Performing Arts (Music)
- Performing Arts (Theatre)
- Visual Arts (Art Museums, Galleries, etc.)
- Community Cultural (Science Museum, Public Radio, etc.)
- Demographic and/or Psychographic

The category grouping of like with like was crucial to the success of the model. Individual trade list segments were often too small to be statistically meaningful on their own, and categorization offered large enough samples for good statistical precision. Although demographics and psychographic data showed little impact when employed in the predictive model, simple distance (how far away from the Symphony did they live) was a highly effective variable.

While summary variables were included in the model (total subscriptions, total single tickets) the segments were most often defined by differences in behavior across individual categories. Apparently, cross-buying activity is an excellent indicator of future loyalty and purchase likelihood. Otherwise, the predictive model would simply mimic the RFM (Recency/Frequency/Monetary) methodology commonly used in direct marketing.

Another advantage to discovering how predictive cross-buying can be, when compared to RFM, is that RFM simply does not work on prospects that have not made a prior donation or purchase. However, the predictive model based on behavior worked quite well among both patrons and prospects, even if the prospects have only been active with another organization.

The predictive model employed created clusters along branches of a tree that can be shown graphically. A typical tree had 50 to 100 or more "Nodes," which are clusters at the end of each branch. It is these end clusters, called "Terminal Nodes," they use to select names.

Rather than show an entire tree, which would cover several pages, sample branches are shown in Exhibit 9.14. The selection is for non-renewing Classical Subscribers. In other words, we are predicting who will buy a Classical Subscription that does not have a current Classical Subscription already. This includes lapsed subscribers, and those who have never subscribed before.

There are several selections and qualifiers prior to the sample branches shown. The selections shown are not the only selections required to determine which Node people are in, but do serve to explain the concept.

The first branch shows 7,143 patrons with an expected overall response of 2.28 percent. There are 1,088 that bought a Classical Subscription less than two years ago. That is Node 6, and expected response is 6.53 percent. The 6,055 people who did not buy a Classical Subscription in the last two years have an expected response of 1.52 percent.

Of the 6,055 people remaining, 1,675 bought a Classical Single in the last two years. That is Node 12, and they are expected to respond at a 2.87 percent rate. The 4,380 who have not bought a Classical Single in the last three years are expected to respond at a 1.0 percent rate.

Of the 4,380 people remaining, 678 have made a donation to the Symphony in the last two years. That is Node 18, and they are expected to respond at a 1.92 percent rate. That leaves 3,702 people remaining. The 727 that have bought two or more Pops tickets in the past are expected to respond at a 1.65 percent rate, and the 2,975 that did not are expected to respond at a 0.64 percent rate.

A similar portion of the tree is shown in Exhibit 9.15, where Trade lists played an impact. Of the 35,470 names in total, expected to respond at an overall rate of 0.09 percent, 3,958 had made a donation in the last year. They are expected to respond at a 0.33 percent rate.

That leaves 31,512 names with an expected response rate of 0.06 per-

Exhibit 9.14: Sample Tree Branch One

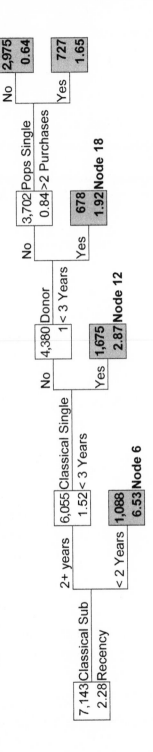

Exhibit 9.15: Sample Tree Branch Two

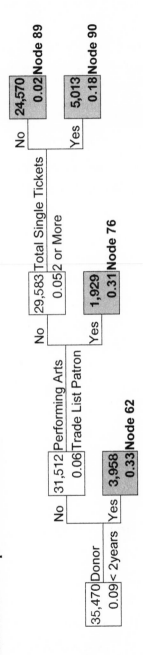

cent. The 1,929 found on a Performing Arts trade list are expected to respond at a 0.33 percent rate, the 29,583 that are not are expected to respond at a 0.05 percent rate. Finally, the 5,013 that have bought two or more single tickets are expected to respond at a 0.18 percent rate, and the 24,570 that did not are expected to respond at only a 0.02 percent rate.

In the end, the marketer has a graphical depiction of what activities in which combinations correlate to response, along with a predicted response by segment.

Name Selection and Contact Strategy

The predictive model created an output very different from the Name Inventory Report. In addition to the tree explained in the prior section, the Gains Chart in Exhibit 9.16 was produced.

The Gains Chart describes how many names are in each "Terminal Node," and described the expected response rate. A marketer can simply look at the Gains Chart and use it to make list selections. Since the response rate is predicted, it is relatively easy to make financial decisions as to who should or should not be contacted.

Notice how responses tend to come from a small portion of the list. For a Classical Subscription for the example symphony, about a 0.20% response rate is required for acceptable financial results. That corresponds to about 120,000 names, far less than the total of 788,239 names they could contact.

Campaign Results

As a test, 175,000 people were contacted using a combination of Nodes and Source. After eliminating current subscribers and people who asked not to be contacted, there were 91,164 names in Nodes with a predicted response rate higher than 0.20%. They were contacted along with 83,836 people selected from the List Inventory Report. This added up to

Exhibit 9.16: Gains Chart

Target Variable: "New" Classical Subscribers   Excludes: Current Classical Subscribers

Node	Count in Node	Node % Overall	Cum # of Prospecs	Cum % of Prospects	Responders by Node	Resp Rate % by Node	Cum # of Responders	Cum % of Responders
6	1,088	0.14	1,088	0.14%	71	6.53%	71	4.74%
22	726	0.09	1,814	0.23%	36	4.96%	107	7.15%
10	1,337	0.17	3,151	0.40%	56	4.19%	163	10.89%
16	1,332	0.17	4,483	0.57%	43	3.23%	206	13.76%
12	1,675	0.21	6,158	0.78%	48	2.87%	254	16.97%
28	1,526	0.19	7,684	0.97%	33	2.16%	287	19.17%
26	1,814	0.23	9,498	1.20%	38	2.09%	325	21.70%
9	1,122	0.14	10,620	1.35%	23	2.05%	348	23.23%
83	1,137	0.14	11,757	1.49%	23	2.02%	371	24.77%
18	678	0.09	12,435	1.58%	13	1.92%	384	25.64%
64	866	0.11	13,301	1.69%	16	1.85%	400	26.71%
42	1,693	0.21	14,994	1.90%	29	1.71%	429	28.64%
24	727	0.09	15,721	1.99%	12	1.65%	441	29.44%
70	968	0.12	16,689	2.12%	13	1.34%	454	30.31%
30	2,455	0.31	19,144	2.43%	32	1.30%	486	32.44%
46	1,099	0.14	20,243	2.57%	14	1.27%	500	33.37%
78	788	0.10	21,031	2.67%	10	1.27%	510	34.04%
50	1,980	0.25	23,011	2.92%	23	1.16%	533	35.57%
74	1,570	0.20	24,581	3.12%	17	1.08%	550	36.70%
100	6,060	0.77	30,641	3.89%	63	1.04%	613	40.91%
86	1,781	0.23	32,422	4.11%	17	0.95%	630	42.04%
58	3,250	0.41	35,672	4.53%	29	0.89%	659	43.97%
36	1,837	0.23	37,509	4.76%	16	0.87%	675	45.04%
87	1,294	0.16	38,803	4.92%	11	0.85%	686	45.77%
15	2,264	0.29	41,067	5.21%	19	0.84%	705	47.04%
44	1,118	0.14	42,185	5.35%	9	0.81%	714	47.64%
38	1,199	0.15	43,384	5.50%	9	0.75%	723	48.24%
23	2,975	0.38	46,359	5.88%	19	0.64%	742	49.51%
97	2,443	0.31	48,802	6.19%	15	0.61%	757	50.51%
93	1,308	0.17	50,110	6.36%	8	0.61%	765	51.04%
45	10,276	1.30	60,386	7.66%	58	0.56%	822	54.88%
54	3,187	0.40	63,573	8.07%	13	0.41%	835	55.76%
85	4,198	0.53	67,771	8.60%	17	0.40%	852	56.88%
99	4,474	0.57	72,245	9.17%	18	0.40%	870	58.07%
77	4,590	0.58	76,835	9.75%	18	0.39%	888	59.27%
104	1,120	0.14	77,955	9.89%	4	0.36%	892	59.54%
62	3,958	0.50	81,913	10.39%	13	0.33%	905	60.41%
76	1,929	0.24	83,842	10.64%	6	0.31%	911	60.81%
95	8,947	1.14	92,789	11.77%	26	0.29%	937	62.54%
96	8,410	1.07	101,199	12.84%	24	0.29%	961	64.17%
116	1,484	0.19	102,683	13.03%	4	0.27%	965	64.43%
35	4,854	0.62	107,537	13.64%	13	0.27%	978	65.31%
110	1,599	0.20	109,136	13.85%	4	0.25%	982	65.58%
72	2,540	0.32	111,676	14.17%	6	0.24%	988	65.98%
88	7,273	0.92	118,949	15.09%	16	0.22%	1,004	67.05%
90	5,013	0.64	123,962	15.73%	9	0.18%	1,013	67.65%
66	9,095	1.15	133,057	16.88%	16	0.18%	1,030	68.75%
92	3,992	0.51	137,049	17.39%	6	0.15%	1,036	69.15%
84	24,923	3.16	161,972	20.55%	27	0.11%	1,063	70.98%
37	909	0.12	162,881	20.66%	1	0.11%	1,064	71.04%
117	204,114	25.89	366,995	46.56%	225	0.11%	1,289	86.03%
57	5,245	0.67	372,240	47.22%	5	0.10%	1,294	86.38%
98	9,647	1.22	381,887	48.45%	8	0.08%	1,302	86.90%
109	85,084	10.79	466,971	59.24%	68	0.08%	1,370	91.44%
108	11,455	1.45	478,426	60.70%	8	0.07%	1,378	91.98%
65	18,644	2.37	497,070	63.06%	9	0.05%	1,387	92.60%
71	14,357	1.82	511,427	64.88%	7	0.05%	1,394	93.08%
115	91,602	11.62	603,029	76.50%	46	0.05%	1,440	96.13%
118	11,140	1.41	614,169	77.92%	4	0.04%	1,445	96.43%
107	97,813	12.41	711,982	90.33%	29	0.03%	1,474	98.39%
89	24,570	3.12	736,552	93.44%	5	0.02%	1,479	98.72%
114	25,513	3.24	762,065	96.68%	5	0.02%	1,484	99.06%
106	26,174	3.32	788,239	100.00%	5	0.02%	1,489	99.41%
	788,239				1,489			

Exhibit 9.17: 2004 Test Results, First Campaign

	Predictive Model	Hand-Picked Segments
Names Mailed	91,164	83,836
% of Mailing	52%	48%
Responders	219	29
Response rate	0.24%	0.03%
% of Responses	88.31%	11.69%
Sales in Dollars	$148,331	$13,913
Sales per Contact	$1.63	$0.17
Cost of Campaign	$45,582	$41,918
Profit/(Loss)	$102,749	($28,005)

the same quantity, 175,000 as mailed the prior year for the same campaign. (See Exhibit 9.17.)

The Nodes represented 52 percent of the mailing, and 88 percent of the response. Sales averaged $1.63 for every contact for the selected Nodes, and only 17 cents for the test names. In other words, the segments not selected in Nodes did not gather enough revenue to cover their postage.

Ten percent more responders came from the 91,164 names contacted in 2004, than came from the 174,228 names contacted in 2003. It was particularly amazing that in 2003, the same mail quantity "missed" 84 people that were in the 700,000-name database, were not on the mail list, but still bought a subscription. The patent-pending methodology "missed" only 27 people, demonstrating how well the model selects people in otherwise low-responding segments.

Of the segments contacted but not selected by the predictive model, none had a response rate above 0.2 percent, and none had enough sales to break-even against mailing costs.

Based on results, a chart was created showing revenue per contact vs. break-even (Exhibit 9.18). The Nodes above about 0.2 percent predicted response performed above break-even, those below 0.2 percent were contacted at a loss.

Exhibit 9.18: Revenue per Contact vs. Break-Even

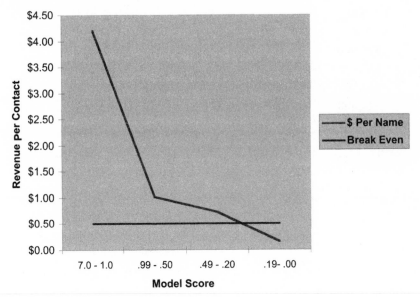

The responses show that some names can be reached at a profit, and some only at a loss. The Predictive Model did a very effective job of predicting which names should (and should not) be contacted.

Overall results showed how the symphony's large campaigns broke even in the past, even when most of the names contacted are expected to be at a loss. Exhibit 9.19 shows Cumulative Profit, based on how many names are selected. This assumes the "best" names are contacted first. After about 90,000 names, the additional names start losing money. However, it takes along time to drive the campaign down to overall break even.

At between 300,000 and 400,000, the overall campaign produces zero profit. Probably not by coincidence, the Symphony in the case study had in the past contacted as many as 350,000 names for prior sub-scription campaigns.

The example shown is based on a single campaign, but the data can be used for a series of campaigns as well. Generally speaking, follow-up contacts get about 50 percent (that's just a rule of thumb) of the first

Exhibit 9.19: Profit/Loss by Mailing Size

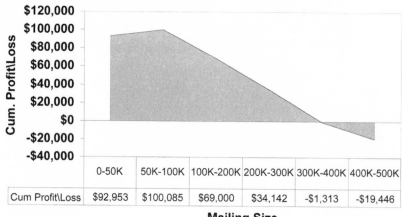

	0-50K	50K-100K	100K-200K	200K-300K	300K-400K	400K-500K
Cum Profit\Loss	$92,953	$100,085	$69,000	$34,142	-$1,313	-$19,446

Mailing Size

contact. A marketer can use the data to select the names for the first campaign, then create a later campaign to re-contact non-responders. By approximately doubling the required expected response rate, profitable re-contacting efforts can be created. This re-contacting of profitable names can further increase overall profitability.

In some cases the Symphony printed many more pieces than the predictive selected as viable targets. They tested the model by mailing the extra pieces and found results were not enough to pay for the postage. In other cases, they threw ten of thousands of pieces away rather than lose money mailing them. As a result, they've learned that their segmentation should be in place before campaign planning occurs, so quantities can be estimated properly in advance.

This symphony has substantially reduced marketing expenses and still increased revenue. Dropping mail quantities from 350,000 two years ago, to 175,000 one year ago year, to finding even better results with 91,000, they have made substantial improvements with just one campaign. Organization-wide, documented improvements exceed $500,000 a year. Marketing campaigns are dramatically smaller (and less expensive) with a similar overall revenue result compared to larger (and much more expensive) campaigns.

In short, improved knowledge from better use of the database resulted in the following changes:

1. Instead of one very large new-buyer acquisition campaign that marginally broke-even or had a loss, the symphony now conducts a series of smaller, profitable campaigns.

2. Marketers can identify and reach prospects they could not previously identify. The process can find a handful of good prospects from a poorly performing list that would otherwise be ignored.

3. Demographic and psychographic names have been virtually eliminated in favor of lists based on behavior gathered through list trades.

Index

A

ABT, see Advocate-Buyer-Tryer
Access, see Software
Acquisition, 233, 234
  Channel(s), 17, 23, 24, 25, 26, 27,
    29, 30, 34
  Cost(s), 71–72, 105–106, 115,
    165
Adoption hurdles, 214–215, 219
Advocate(s), 40–41, 48, 49, 58, 64,
    65, 66, 93–94, 100, 101,
    123–124, 136, 151, 154, 156,
    159, 160, 215
Advocate-Buyer-Tryer (ABT), 93,
    100–101
Analysis, 38, 57, 59, 91, 93, 101,
    121–122, 129, 130, 131, 132,
    133, 160, 171, 229, 231, 241,
    242–244, 248, 251
  Advertising space analysis, see
    Square Inch Report
  Advocates-Buyers-Tryer (ABT)
    analysis, 93, 94, 100
  Area analysis, 47
  Break-even analysis, 85
  Cluster analysis, 53–55, 92,
    245–248, 246
    Dynamic cluster analysis, 54
    Static cluster analysis, 53
  Cross-tab analysis, 41–43, 93
  Descriptive analysis, 55
  Inventory analysis, 49
  Marketing analysis, 91

Multi-channel performance
    analysis, 57–58
Predictive modeling analysis, 91
Progression of, 122–127
RFM analysis, 93–94
RFA analysis, 94
Regression analysis, 50, 92
SWOT analysis, 30
Segmentation analysis, 142–144
Situation analysis
    Initial review, 180–182
    Step One: Employ database
      marketing methodology,
      182–185
    Step Two: Load data, 185–186
    Step Three: Data check,
      186–188
    Step Four: Data hygiene,
      188–190
    Step Five: Set data dictionary,
      190–191
    Step Six: Create reports
      describing data, 191–195
    Step Seven: Data mining,
      195–199
    Step Eight: Exploring and
      defining relationships,
      199–200
    Step Nine: Create descriptive
      statistics, 200–202
    Step Ten: Predictive and
      descriptive modeling,
      202–204

271

About TEXERE

Texere, a progressive and authoritative voice in business publishing, brings to the global business community the expertise and insights of leading thinkers. Our books educate, enlighten, and entertain, and provide an intersection where our authors and our readers share cutting edge ideas, practices, and innovative solutions. Texere seeks to cultivate, enhance, and disseminate information that illuminates the global business landscape.

www.thomson.com/learning/texere

About the typeface

This book was set in 11 pt Times Roman. Times Roman is a body text, serified typeface. This typeface is known for its readability and economical use of space.

Library of Congress Cataloging-in-Publication Data

Weber, Alan.
    Data-driven business models / Alan Weber.
       p. cm.
    1. Marketing—Data processing. 2. Marketing—Economic models.
3. Business planning. I. Title.
    HF5415.125.W39 2005
    658.8′01′5195—dc22

2005015640